MW00933337

REDWOOD TO DEADWOOD:

A 53-YEAR OLD DUDE HITCHHIKES ACROSS AMERICA. AGAIN.

By

COLIN FLAHERTY

RedwoodToDeadwoodBook.com

Cover design by Terry Lynch
Book design by Book International D

Printed in the United States of America
First Printing: September 2011
Second Edition, May 2012
ISBN-13:
978-1477674055
ISBN-10:
1477674055

The Critics on Colin Flaherty

"Colin Flaherty is a strong favorite."

David Ignatius
Washington Post Columnist.
New York Times Best Selling Author

"Colin Flaherty is one of the best reporters I've ever worked with. "

Christi Dunn
Former Editor
San Diego Business Journal

The Critics on Redwood to Deadwood:

"Great book by a great guy."

NPR

"This is a lighthearted and entertaining read about a 53-year-old writer who decided to hitchhike around America for three months. The book offers some interesting insights into the lives of the many people who gave him a ride, and demonstrates there are still friendly people in this country willing to give a stranger a ride. The author, Colin Flaherty, is an award-winning writer."

Top Ten Adventure Travel Book
About.com

"Hitchhiking books fit better in a genre of alternative travel books, with Jack Kerouac's On The Road, Bill Bryson's A Walk in the Woods and Robert Pirsig's Zen and the Art of Motorcycle Maintenance. To that list of fun and funny and moving and important books, we should add Colin Flaherty's *Redwood to Deadwood, a 53-year old dude hitchhikes across America. Again.*" --

hitchwiki.org

"Great book by a great American writer."

J. Stryker Meyer, #1 Amazon best selling author

"This 53-year old award-winning writer stuck out his thumb, and sticking to the back roads and curvy twists on the map (a la Pirsig) he spent the next three months zig zagging around to places where the closest Wal-Mart is 120 miles away.

"These places still exist. Great characters still live there. And in *Redwood to Deadwood*, a great writer tells us all about them.

"I've had a lot of fun reading this book. And so have my friends. And I hope you do too."

Pottstown Mercury

Hitchhiking? Who the heck does that any more anyway? The guy was 53-years old for Cripes sakes. The book is half Keroauc, half Dave Barry, and half whoever your favorite 'moving' author is.

That's too many halves, isn't it? Oh well. This book will make you lose track of what you thought you knew.

Funny how The Boss never got around to writing a song about hitchhiking. If he reads this book, he probably will.

The writing is top notch. **He not only makes you feel as if you are there, he makes you feel that you want to be there. And the part of the book where he hitchhikes to**

meet the people who were with his brother when he died in Viet Nam is not to be missed.

I don't even know if there is a genre of hitchhiking books out there. But this is **the best hitchhiking I have ever read or even heard about**.

Asbury Park Pilot

"The book *Deadwood to Redwood* is amazing, I loved reading every page of it, I love seeing how other people experience the country because its different for everyone.

"Its also great to read the book to see just how many people actually pick up hitch hickers,

"While I'm sure that the author being able to sleep in hotel rooms made quite a difference in the amount of people willing to pick him up (most hitchhikers from my expereience don't have this luxury)

"I really loved meeting all the people that Colin met in the book, I adored reading his thoughts about them, taking his own life experiences into it, the trip to Canada is sure to have you laughing.

"If you haven't traveled the country, or even if you have this book is a great way to get a feel for it.

Megan at mommypants12.com

It has an usual combination of humor and pathos and adventure that the author, Colin Flaherty, experienced during his recent three-month trip where he hitchhiked across the United States.

Hitchhiking? Who the heck does that any more anyway? The guy was 53-years-old for cripes sake. The book is half Kerouac, half

Dave Barry, and half whoever your favorite “moving” author is. That’s too many halves, isn’t it? Oh well.

It was one of the most unusual and satisfying books our club ever read. We liked it.

Green Valley Arizona News

Now that's an adventure. Thumbs up.

Discovery Channel

Chapter 1

Day One: On My Way to the Robbery in Steamboat.

Let's get this party started

My first day on the road and I got robbed in Steamboat Springs.

The day started out with promise enough. My neighbor in Dillon, Colorado got all excited when I told him I was going to hitchhike around the country and write a book about it.

"A journey of self-discovery," Mike said, nodding in approval, as I loaded my small pack into the back of his Subaru.

"No," I said so quickly it must have seemed snappish. "This is not going to be some kind of thumb-sucking journey into the back ways of my mind."

I did not know why I objected so vigorously to anyone thinking I might actually learn something about myself after such an adventure.

But then, I did not now know before I tucked my thumb in for the final time, I'd almost get killed, chase wild horses, visit a pot plantation, get into crazy family feuds, restart my business, ride in cop cars, hunt big game, poach big game, get chased by a helicopter, reconnect with old friends, make new ones, get tired and exhilarated and lost and found and scorned and accepted, kicked out and invited in.

That and a lot more. I now know how to cook muskrat, squirrel and rockchucks.

Had I known, I would not have said anything so stupid to Mike.

Though I felt as if I had slightly chastised him, he was big enough and smart enough and wise enough to ignore it. That's a lot more of that out there than I realized before the big trip.

It seemed important at the time that I did not want to sound like some earth shoe wearing child of the universe waiting for the next Dead revival. I was a 53-year old guy with a few notches on his belt: I had spent the previous 32 years in California, where I had arrived hitchhiking in 1976.

Married. Divorced. Two kids. Grown. Political staffer. Opposition researcher. Speech writer. Column writer. Journalist. Hundreds of appearances on TV and radio, some local, some national. Marketing guru to major companies. And for five months in the winter after all of that, a snowboard instructor near Vail, Colorado.

DILLON TO STEAMBOAT MAP.

I wanted to hold on to that. But all of a sudden, in December of 2008, I was living in a world where solid things slipped away. I was bored. And nothing begets desperation like a bit of boredom.

So I decided to write about something else that slipped away: Hitchhiking.

Mike on the Mountain

"You ought to get everyone to tell you their best story," Mike said. "Watch out for my mountain gear. I use it for Search and Rescue."

Now that sounded like a story. "What's your best one?" I asked him. And with a bit of prodding he told me as we drove past Dillon Lake, where the chair sank through the ice just a few days before; putting a few hundred dollars into the pocket of a lucky local.

"I've seen more avalanches and plane crashes than anyone in the country. I've been a member of mountain search and rescue for 30 years. So a while back we got a call to rescue a hiker stranded near a mountain top in a thunder storm. Instead of approaching from below, we figured out it would be better to come at her from the other side of the mountain, over the top and down to her."

"As we reached the peak, really more of mesa no more than 20 yards around, the weather shifted and soon the lightning clouds were right on top of us. Then lightning started to strike all around and I knew I was going to die.

"One of the other guys started cursing at the top of his lungs. Later I learned it was a Howard Stern routine. The other guy started walking in circles, knowing the lightning could not strike him if he kept moving.

"I fell to my knees and started praying."

And he put his hands together and pointed his fingers to the sky with a fervor I had not seen since First Holy Communion. Mine.

"During that one minute lightning struck six times. When it stopped, we still had a job to do so we called in a rescue helicopter from the base near Vail. Soon it was hovering over our position when a blast of wind picked it up and turned it vertical. I thought it was going to flip over and crash. It didn't."

"As soon as he recovered control of the aircraft, he told us on the radio that he was returning to base and he said it so calmly you might have thought he was telling us he was heading down to City Market to get a loaf of bread."

"Finally we reached the girl and the rain and clouds were so thick we could barely see in front of us. We got a bit unhappy with her when she started telling us how to get her down from the mountain."

Ah, the vicious head of unjustified self regard. I recognized it right away. Some folks, no matter how life or circumstances humble them, never acquire that dose of humility that allows them to learn from it.

Any book on writing will tell you that high self regard is an essential tool in the writer's kit. As I told aspiring writers when I taught a class on research and writing at the University of California San Diego.

"Any egomaniacs in the room?" I asked.

Not a hand stirred.

"Each one of you would like to someday write a story then tell 400,000 neighbors they should make that an important part of their day. Does that sound like healthy ego development?"

The bobble heads bobbled side to side.

Journalism, it is said, the art of writing with absolute authority about something you know nothing about.

The clueless hiker had that kind of mojo. She probably has a book deal, an Oprah appearance, and a New York Times weekly column by now.

Little did I know that in a few short hours that same self regard would crush me like a can of crushed worms.

For the first time, but not the last, I looked at the person giving me a ride and marveled that we had some great and humble people hiding in plain sight everywhere you go.

Mike sent me on my way with a wistful, encouraging look and a fist pump, which I took as a grand omen.

When a 53-year old guy tells his friends he is leaving for a two-month hitchhiking trip around the country, you get two reactions: 1) Take a knife; 2) Wow, that's great! Followed by a fist pump.

Knives and fists aside, I had a robbery to catch in Steamboat Springs.

Turns out taking a knife would have been the worst thing I could have done.

THE LOOMING SIDEWALK

There it was: My first spot, looming a hundred yards away. A sidewalk. I glued my eyes to my first jump off point and considered my options.

This was stupid. Nobody was going to pick me up. I cannot remember the last time I even saw a hitchhiker. What the hell was I doing there?

75 yards.

I could always turn around. Just turn around. Only I had nowhere to go. On both sides of the street, shoppers were coming and going from small stores with food and clothing and knick knacks for the coming Spring. No one noticed.

Snow coated the mountain tops and littered the ground. May 3, 2009: Too early to declare the end of winter just yet.

But I wanted to see the Spring at somewhere below the 9100 feet where I had just spent the last five months.

50 yards.

Of all the stupid ideas I ever had, this was the most stupid. I looked around for a way out.

I flashed back to Rehoboth Beach 1971. I was hitchhiking home to catch my shift as a dishwasher at Mr. Steak. Pat Mulvena drove by, picked me up, and took me back to Rehoboth.

"We're having too much fun for you to go home. Forget that dishwashing job. You're staying here."

I did. He was right.

I looked around again: Pat and his VW bug were not going to rescue me now.

There was no way back.

25 yards.

I knew I had to start sliding my pack off my shoulders and slow down. Or else I would just keep walking.

5 yards.

I slide my small pack to the sidewalk and turned around. One thing left to do. Panic, mildly. Then put out my thumb for the first time.

Nobody's going to pick me up and besides, I feel kind of stupid. I'm 53-years old with a career where I make pretty good money – at least until the world stopped a few months ago – and I have a nice family – at least I did until my 20-something kids decided to do their angry teen thing on me about ten years behind schedule. I was absolutely sure it could not have been my fault.

But I was kind of bored. It first came on me about 10 months before. I was on the 11 hole of a golf course at a private country club that cost $350,000 to join and where I was a guest every weekend. We teed off around 9 a.m. and I could not remember the last time we had to wait, or even the last time we had anyone playing in front or behind us.

I drove a nice car. Had a nice good looking girlfriend.

"I'm bored," I told my buddy and client Mick. "I wouldn't mind finding something to do outside of San Diego."

A few months later, the financial tsunami left all my once and future clients underwater. I'm the kind of person who thinks consultants are no good if their clients go out of business.

So there I was. Condemned to the road by my own words.

With nothing better to do, I packed up as much stuff as I could in my 10 year old Jaguar XK8 and sold the rest. I felt a little like Ghengis Khan and his Mongols, riding my horse as far as it would go, then eating it.

With worried looks from family and friends, I headed out to Vail, Colorado to spend the winter snowboarding.

Soon I was teaching it, with 20 other guys and women, most less than half my age.

I didn't really have a good answer to the unspoken question I faced every day: 'What are you doing here?" One of my buddies wanted to know if I was in the witness protection program.

No, I was in the boredom prevention program.

So I put down my pack and stuck out my thumb.

I had decided that the key to getting rides was presenting a non-threatening, clean cut picture on the road. Maybe I could try to look fun and interesting too. So those were the vibes I was putting out when the first (of many) cops drove by.

I straightened up. Then it struck me: Even if it cost me a few rides, I do not want people to think I am some toothless hound dog sitting by the fire. I'm dangerous dammit. I could jaywalk at any minute.

Then I remembered the travel writer's motto: Bad travel makes good writing. And I knew what I had to do if the cop came over and started the whole search me, question me routine.

That's what they do, right? Hell, I had no idea about that or anything else I would find out on the road. I had not begged anyone for a ride in 32 years -- back then I had hitched 30,000 miles in several trips all over the country.

I decided I was going to look that cop right in the eye and repeat my favorite John Rambo line: "Why you pushin' me?"

I had no intentions of burning a small town to the ground. But if it happened I'd probably have some pretty interesting stories to tell from the chain gang where they put desperados like Rambo and me.

But today there would be no dumping my stuff on the side of the road while he inspected it with a billy club and smirk. No such luck.

He just kept going, probably didn't even see me any more than he would notice the old hound dog. Cops are too damn nice. Another obstacle on my road to great travel writing.

THE FIRST RIDE.

My disappointment in the atrociously courteous behavior of the local constables soon dissipated when a Red Jeep pulled over and waved me in.

This was it. My first ride.

Within 15 minutes Tim and I were talking as if we had known each other for 15 years. Family. Business. Home. Kids. Books. Rugby.

"I'm hitchhiking around the country and writing a book on it," I said for the first of about 300 times. "And this is my first ride."

"Cool," said Tim. And we got back to gabbing. I told him how I was going where my rides took me, staying on the back roads when I could. A 'Zen and the Art of Motorcycle Maintenance' kind of thing.

I carried a small Swiss Army back pack that was stuffed with 25 pounds of shirts, a computer and a copy of Atlas Shrugged. I'm one of those crazy people who picked up the newspaper every day and thought the gang in power were doing some kind of weird parody of the famous Ayn Rand novel.

Only they never figured out who the bad guys were. The pack was just big enough to fit the computer.

Soon we were 30 minutes from Tim's home in Steamboat.

"You really don't know where you are going, do you?" said Tim.

"After Rushmore, not really," I said. "Though I might go up and visit one of my brother's friends in North Dakota."

I had not thought of that 'till that instant.

"My brother died in Viet Nam and this guy was with him when it happened. I made a video out of it a few years ago but he was not around. They named a landing zone after him and all that. Sorry, I did not mean to be overemotional or anything."

I do not usually talk to people about personal tragedies a few minutes after first meeting them. But I also knew that if I was going to have any fun on this trip, I would have to be a lot more open to strangers and everyone else.

That meant saying hello to people on the street, even if they were staring at the sidewalk when we passed. Engaging a city bus driver if I needed help getting through the bad side of town. Staying off the freeways and sticking to the side roads where the small towns live,

But Tim was eager to hear about my brother, so I told him. Then he said: "You should stay at my house tonight. You can take my car and go visit the mud baths and hot springs. You'll love it."

Wow. This hitchhiking thing was a breeze. And staying in Steamboat sounded like fun but I did suggest he might want to ask his lovely bride. "Bringing hitchhikers to a home with a wife and two kids is not something you would expect a wife to understand."

Nor should you really. Things had not changed that much since 1976, my last big cross country hitchhiking excursion.

A few minutes later Tim's wife was on the phone, reminding him of some domestic responsibility that may have slipped his mind and we soon parted in downtown Steamboat as friends.

You never forget your first.

STEAMBOAT, AT LAST.

What a cool and clean place, Steamboat is. With lots of interesting sculptures. Not the kind of town where a stranger expects to be robbed of his most important possession.

But that is what happened just a few hours after entering the "Off the Beaten Path" bookstore and coffee shop.

It started out, innocently enough, with a flyer in a window. Which is also how I eventually met my ex-wife. Ignore warnings from the universe at your own peril.

The flyer announced that very evening this very bookstore would be holding a poetry slam and anyone could enter. As long as they had a few original poems, that is.

"What the hell was a poetry slam," I wondered.

I had no idea. But I knew I had to enter. Probably because I knew I was going to win. Self regard, flying high. I had published several poems in English and Spanish back in my college days, so what the heck.

I had three hours to write four poems. So after dismissing the idea of going into the stacks and stealing a few paragraphs from e.e. cummings (and no one, not even the rain, has such small hands…) I got to work. I put away my Ayn Rand, grabbed a cup of java (that's what we poets call it, java…) and , outside on one of their tables, started to scribble.

A girl in green dress walked by. She smiled. Down by the river a block away, I saw some swallows. A train full of coal rolled through downtown Steamboat, reminding me that before this trip was over, after I became the poetry champ of Steamboat, I wanted to hop a train.

By 7 O'clock I was ready. I gave my poems a once over and knew I was going to win. Dominate.

Of the 15 poets, a random drawing placed me at the end. For the remainder of the evening, the other contestants would call me "The Last Poet."

There would be two rounds where we each had three minutes to do our thing, with three finalists competing at the end.

The first guy, the First Poet, Ceasar, talked about dead cats and his girlfriend's feet. I did not hear any rhymes or meter but I'm probably old fashioned that way. Besides, next to the word orange, poets know that it is just about impossible to rhyme anything with "rubbing her feet."

Look it up.

I had been standing next to him in the coffee line a few moments before and Ceasar was holding forth with some passion about the international bankers. I was looking forward to hearing a poem about that, but he soon finished without it.

I led the applause from the back of the room. The 20 or so spectators joined in. I've always taken some pride in my ability to get a roomful of people clapping.

My confidence grew as Carl took the stage and adjusted the mike. He looked and sounded like the Unabomber.

When his three minutes were up I led the applause and started planning what I was going to do with my new found status as winner of the Steamboat Poetry Slam.

Soon the girls started their reading from what could have been called "Bad Boyfriends On Parade." F-bombs filled the air like lightning on a mountain rescue. These girls were pissed. If they ever hear that I called them girls they will probably be reaming me out in three minute bursts for the next 27 years.

I led the applause and noticed how Crissy the Angry Chick Poet had a nice, thin neck and happy, sexy demeanor -- for an angry chick.

I dwelled on her neck for a while, noting blood runs hot in the poetry profession.

My self regard inflated like a porno doll. Dave stood up and talked about his friend the drug addict. He said something about something "nestling in his nostrils." I clapped.

Joey and others talked about more drugs and dragons.

Finally it came to me. The plan: Open friendly and fun and save the big guns for the second round.

"This is a poem about literary smack downs," I said. "And I'd like to dedicate it to all the poets out there." I looked at the girl with the long neck. And smiled.

After one minute the Last Poet returned to his seat. The applause was probably deafening. Though as I walked through the cheering throng I was too busy preparing my Pulitzer Prize poetry application to take much notice.

You want a sample, don't you? Well, I don't know ... How about the title, that should be enough: "Damn Slam."

Said in much the same way you would say Damn Jack if Jack had indeed just hit a grand slam in some baseball game.

See: Told you. The boxing and sports metaphor was brilliant, I hear you thinking. After all it was combat. How perceptive of you to notice how cool that it was that I figured it out. It was goo---ood.

Goodbye marketing communications. Hello poetry professor with all the nubile fringe benefits so important to working poets. Want to start a violent revolution on every campus in America? Tell college professors they cannot fraternize with the nubile co-eds.

The second round was pretty much the same as the first. Dead cats and bad boyfriends. With a smattering of girlfriends' feet and dragon's teeth.

I floated to the mike to accept my accolades. But first I had to take care of a few formalities, like reading my poems. So after telling the awe-struck crowd that I had written a few poems about Steamboat and "was there anyone there who lived in Steamboat?" I began.

But not before noting that the long necked poet was smiling.

Inspired by T.S. Elliott. Richard Brautigan. Ferlinghetti. I mixed them all up and sprinkled them in a literary stew over my competitors.

I would have used e.e. cummings had it occurred to me. And if it occurs to you that sprinkling a stew over an appreciative audience might not be the best use of that metaphor, then you have a lot to learn about poetry. So back off.

I felt their minds opening in appreciation. The Last Poet finished, floating back to his chair on a gauzy cloud of self regard. The Last Poet prepared for the finals. I contemplated the private poetry lessons I would give to Long Neck.

Five minutes later, they announced the finalists. And it took me a lifetime squeezed into 10 seconds to realize, The Last Poet did not make the Final Cut.

ROBBERY!

But I stayed. I clapped. I put on a happy, even brave, face.

The guy who waxed poetic on nostrils won. My prize, that is.

I congratulated the victors and talked to my competitors. Surely they were going to console me with their outrage at the poetic injustice we had all just witnessed.

Didn't happen.

LIARS!

Long Neck said I was funny. Which was fine by me, but that was about it. There would be no poetry lessons, no intimate literary appreciations in Steamboat Springs that night. No one really knew who I was, or what I was doing there. The next day, I would pretty much tell anyone I met when I was wearing my backpack about my mission. But not then.

Calm down. I know you want a sample of the literary gems that were so undervalued that sad night.

Here: read it for yourself. Not to judge. To appreciate.

Girls in green on 4th street.
Guys in boots on 5th.
They clatter and chatter and
Ask 'what's the matter."

I forgot there was some Springsteen in there too. And a few lines later:

Down by the river
the swallows come and go,
chirping of Michealangelo."

Told ya. Long Neck liked that one a lot.

For my third poem I thought I'd open a can of Richard Brautigan whup ass on 'em. So I gave the poem about a one minute build up, dedicating it to Tim, talking about how he lived there and what he did. Then I described the poem as a haiku in 97 verses. Which I think I stole my friend Margot on Facebook.

So I cupped my hands over my mouth, megaphone style, and began by shouting out the window:

Hey Tim. Thanks for the lift.

Guess you had to be there.

Chapter 2

Crazy Horse Rushmore Here I Come. Or Buffalo Killers on the Plain.

And say hello to Tony Curtis.

The world's most dangerous buffalo killer didn't seem all that menacing when I hopped in his car on the way to the Crazy Horse Memorial.

We would only travel a few miles together. But by the time we reached Crazy Horse mountain, it became clear to me how he came to be the scourge of buffaloes everywhere, as well as one of the most memorable rides on this meandering trip.

The first ride was Tim. And as you may have seen in my last post, he decided he and his family were going to take me in for the night, lend me their car so I could visit the local hot springs and mud bath, and generally be my best buddies in Steamboat Springs, Colorado.

HITCHHIKING BACK IN THE DAY.

During my 30,000 miles of hitchhiking in the early 70's, I do not remember the other rides to be quite as accommodating. The fist big hitchhiking trip I ever took was the 1500 miles down to Miami Beach for the Republican National Convention in 1972. I was one of those people convinced that Republicans in general and Nixon in particular were the source of all evil in the history of the planet if not the universe.

The people who gave me a ride then had the same attitude towards me then that I have towards those events now. Bemused.

So down I went, and ended up spending two days in jail with Allen Ginsburg for my troubles. I was in a bookstore recently when a college student came and sat next to me. She was carrying a volume of Great American poets and there was good old Allen glaring at me from the cover. He looked bemused. It's a poet thing.

I was going to try and impress her that Mr. Ginsburg and I were old cellmates --and how -- between meals of Dade County baloney sandwiches and Kool Aid -- he led me and the other miscreants in chanting OOOMMMMMMMMMM.

Or was it OMMMMMMMMMMMM. Whatever.

But I decided to forgo this excursion into the literary life with this eager academe. Nothing worse trying to impress a coed with meeting a famous poet in jail and have her either not believe you. Or worse, not care.

Come to think of it, there are millions of things worse.

After two days, the Dade County authorities dropped charges and let us all go. Soon after I called my folks and they asked me how I was doing. "What do you mean" I asked, looking for any opportunity to brag to anyone that I just spent two days in jail. (As you can see that impulse dies hard.)

"Anything happen to you?"

"I just got out of jail."

I think my dad laughed. Though he did not really think it was that funny when a month later a picture of me getting arrested ended up as the cover picture for Hunter Thompson's story in Rolling Stone magazine on the Republican National Convention.

Thirty seven years later I wrote an article for Aspen.com (where Hunter lived) about his life and death. It was not an appreciation.

I was actually going to convert the first few sentences of that Aspen.com article into a poem for the finals of the now-infamous Steamboat Poetry Slam.

Hunter Thompson is dead.

He killed himself 40 years ago
when he figured out

it was a lot easier being a circus
clown with a typewriter,

a bottle of bourbon and

a fistful of drugs instead of being a
writer.

It just took a while.

By now you should know what a mockery cruel fate and even crueler poetry judges made of that ambition.

Hitchhiking was no big deal in the 70's. But almost no one did it now. So I thought it would be fun to see the difference.

I got the hitchhiking bug in tenth grade. Though when I was five years old, I do remember just standing on a busy sidewalk, as my brothers played wiffle ball a few feet away, and sticking my thumb out. Not really knowing why.

On high school weekends some of our gang would cross the Delaware Memorial Bridge to drink in New Jersey. To this day I cannot think of any other reason to go to New Jersey -- outside of Atlantic City, of course.

We piled in cars there and back. Once one of the older guys talked about taking off on a hitchhiking trip to Texas with "$1.71" in his pocket and returning two weeks later with "$15."

Now that sounded adventurous. I knew right then some day I would do something like that. Just like Ricky Barnes. He wore a cowboy hat like one of the Fabulous Furry Freak Brothers. He died of a drug overdose a few years later, wearing the same hat.

About a year or so after my run-in with the law in Miami Beach, I found myself on the road again to Florida. This time headed loosely for Key West. On the way down I met a follower of an early psychotherapist called Wilhelm Reich.

Reich's big contribution was telling everyone we all had this kind of energy called Orgone and that all disease came screwing up this energy through sexual repression.

Hey I had just done 12 years in Catholic schools so no one needed to convince me. Reich spent some time in prison and was hounded out of the shrink profession -- which was kind of hard since there was only about ten of them at the time -- all because of his Theory of the Orgone.

That's how the story went.

Anyway, somehow, his Florida disciple figured out to keep the orgone flowing orgonically, you needed some kind of orgone box. So this guy and I drove to machine shops all over Dade County trying to buy materials so that he could build an orgone box. Which I remember as some kind of pyramid.

I was wondering if Buffalo killer could have used some time in the box.

The early hitchhiking trips were pretty safe. Or I was just too oblivious to know if I was anywhere near danger.

Though one time I started to feel uncomfortable and had to ask about five times the two guys in the front seat to let me out in the middle of the Texas desert. Wasn't sure what they had in mind but I did not stick around to find out.

The only flat out bad ride I ever had was on my way to California in 1974. Two sailors picked me up somewhere in Arizona and let me off in El Centro. Way out in the desert, 2 a.m.

It was the only time during the whole trip I got out of the car in before my bag. And as soon as I got out, they drove off with my pack, laughing in the desert night.

But not before I scribbled their license number down on my palm.

The next day in San Diego, the highway patrol told me over the phone there was nothing they could do. I like cops but let's face it, most of the time you have to deliver a video tape of the crime along with a signed confession before they arrest anyone. Unless of course you are parking on a yellow line in a public lot.

Anyway, the cop gave me their address in San Jose and so I sent them a registered letter, using $2.50 of the remaining $30 I had in my pocket.

The letter thanked them for the ride. But also said "when you stole my pack, you made the worst mistake of your life. Now I am either going to get my pack back or a check for $200, or you will spend Christmas in jail. "(It was the day before Thanksgiving.) Which of course was a big fat lie.

But I got both. Along with a note that began "Dear Mr. Flaherty: You have been the victim of unfortunate human circumstantial behavior."

I don't have the slightest idea what that meant but it went on that way for two pages.

Along with the letter was a check for $200 and my clothes, washed and folded. I think their moms did it.

Case closed.

Those guys could definitely have used some time in the old orgone chamber.

But other than that, and other than the time that nice looking girl picked me up in Houston (gentlemen don't tell) most of the rest of the people were pretty nice.

After being run out of Steamboat Springs by a cadre of great literature- hating citizens as if I were Wilhelm Reich toting an orgone box, I was on the road to Mt. Rushmore.

No particular reason, I just always wanted to go to Rushmore. But somehow I always saw myself getting there riding high in a real nice RV. And on the advice of Tim and my own gut, I decided that was the only way I would ever enter Mt. Rushmore.

But I was feeling lucky enough to make that happen.

EVERYBODY IS DOING SOMETHING OUT HERE.

Holding out my thumb near a Steamboat campground, I took an inventory of my stuff:

Two short sleeve, Booby Jones golfing shirts. One long sleeve white shirt with Nordstrom logo. One Nordstrom sweater. Some underwear. Long underwear. Cologne, of course. A book: Atlas Shrugged. One pair of shoes and one pair of pants, which I was wearing. One computer, which I dropped and was not working. Rogaine. One atlas, which I really didn't need. A notebook.

All stuffed into a small, Swiss Army backpack. It felt as if it weighed around 250 pounds, though it was closer to 35.

No blanket. No sleeping bag. Lots of trepidation, which like the pages of Atlas Shrugged that I ripped out and threw away as soon as I read them to keep the weight down (except for the infamous 75 page 'rant' at the end which I kept,) it diminished more the further along I got.

My first full day on the road: Holding out my thumb near a Steamboat campground, Papaya Man wheeled his pickup truck -- hauling snow plows -- over a mud puddle. I hopped around the water and into the cab.

Papaya Man was ruddy faced guy about my age was happy to have the company as he needed to drive about an hour or so to put his snow equipment in storage and get his lawnmowers out.

He told me about his wife who grew up in the South Pacific and how they were going there next year to live. They had recently bought a farm and planted 10,000 papaya trees there.

Dang. Over the next eight weeks and hundreds of rides, just about every single person would surprise me with something excellent and unusual about their lives. Most of the time, they did not even recognize it as such.

The next ride was my first with a dog. And as we headed North to the Wyoming border, Highway Man pointed to the mountains where he kept a cabin and told me about how he was in charge of road construction for a good portion of that part of the state. His dad, who they called Stoney, was one of Ken Kesey's Merry Pranksters and he spent part of his childhood "on the bus." Meeting all the famous hippies of the day.

Including someone I was supposed to have heard of called Wavy Gravy. Who now had a farm north of San Francisco, a place where I had never been and had no intentions of going. Nor did I have any intentions of almost getting killed by a drug dealer there, but that is what happened.

Like the guy before, Mountain Man was happy and healthy and prosperous and delighted in his son's video productions and native intelligence as well as his own place in the universe.

THE MOST IMPORTANT LESSON IN HITCHHIKING

Here's a hitchhiking lesson. Maybe the most important one: Moods are contagious – and it goes both ways. If you are happy and excited about your life, that will spread. If you start telling stories about bad rides and hard times, that will spread too. And you don't want that.

You don't have to be a Pollyanna, but saying the first thing that pops into your head probably won't work either.

After Highway Man dropped me off, I did not realize till later that he went about 50 miles out of his way to get me to a spot where he knew I would get a lift.

Soon enough, The Last Poet, Nowhere Man, was in the middle of NoWhere, Wyoming. By now, my trepidation was gone, replaced with anticipation, even eagerness, when two young truck drivers pulled over and offered me a place in the back of their beat up old car.

But like every other car I would encounter in the Midwest, cosmetics aside, every car ran smooth and quiet because the owners kept them that way. And they did it effortlessly.

Soon we were on Highway something or other heading East. It did not really bother me that I was violating my own desires to stay on the side roads and off the freeways. For two reasons: One,

Highway 70 is deserted most of the time, except for the antelopes. Two, I was also determined to go where my rides went.

And as soon as I dove into the back seat and moved the clutter over, we just started talking and pretty much didn't stop for a couple of hundred miles. They were curious and so was I.

WADE AND MICHELLE GO THE PROM

They had both just turned 20, and they were returning to their hometown of Buffalo, Wyoming so that Wade could take Michelle to the senior prom. They had just started new jobs as truck drivers on a construction site and they loved driving those big-tired rigs around.

Both were clearly nice kids, but after Wade started talking about how he was raised by his grandparents in Buffalo, I kind of got the impression that he was a bit too feral for the senior prom. So I broached it gently then just jumped in all the way.

At this point I was still wearing my Father of the Year badge, so I offered young people advice freely and with confidence not yet contradicted by experience that would change well before the trip was over.

When I was just a few years older then them, I went to a black tie dinner in a sweater because no one told me anything different. I don't really consider my self an advice-dispensing machine, but every once in a while you just have to tell someone something they need to know.

"Wade, you are going to shave and get a haircut before tomorrow night, right?" His friend the driver laughed. "That'll be the day."

So I pulled my trump: "chicks like guys who clean up in a tux.You gotta get a hair cut. And shave. Another thing: How are your table manners?"

Had there been any blowback, I would have stopped and changed directions: No harm. No foul. But some young guys without dads know they missed something, they just don't know what. Wade was open for it. Or at least amused by it.

But he was also one of the those guys who had never had any trouble getting chicks doing the run-down loner bit, either.

"Here's how you hold a knife and fork," I started as I leaned forward between from the back seat until my hands were holding a pen and pencil between them. "Just don't grab it as if you are on Buffy the Vampire Slayer and about to run it through some body cavity."

And I picked up the pen and chopped it up and down, Psycho style.

"And when you pause for some reason during dinner, you do not put the knife and fork in your pocket; You put them at 4 O'clock and 8 O'clock on your plate. Tines down." And I showed him. "And when you are done, put the knife and fork together, tines down, at four O'Clock." And I showed him that too.

"Hey I never knew that," Wade said.

"Me either," said the driver.

Good Lord they were actually listening. Life lessons from the Hitchhiker dude. The Last Poet.

"Believe me: Chicks notice. I don't care if the chick is high class Beverly Hills, or the world's biggest meth head, they notice."

"And if you want to go Master's Class, check this out: Here's how you butter bread: Take some butter and put it on your bread plate. Break off just enough bread for a small mouthful. Place the butter on your bread and eat the entire piece at once."

"You do that, and could eat dinner and talk corgies with the Queen of England she would never know you are a home-grown wild boy from Wyoming."

One last thing: "And I see people doing this wrong on TV all the time: When a gentleman escorts a lady down the street, the guy walks on the curb side. That goes for Wyoming proms and Manhattan Charity Balls."

Manners lesson over, they told me about growing up in Wyoming. The truck tire donuts in the fields. Guns and mail boxes. Cars, all kinds of things with cars.

Nothing malicious. But they always got caught. Small towns have nowhere to hide.

Small town kids are also desperately bored. Rather than sit around doing nothing, most of them will figure out something. It helps if you know that your parents will hate it. Big town kids too, come to think of it.

Steamboat Springs to Buffalo, Wyoming.

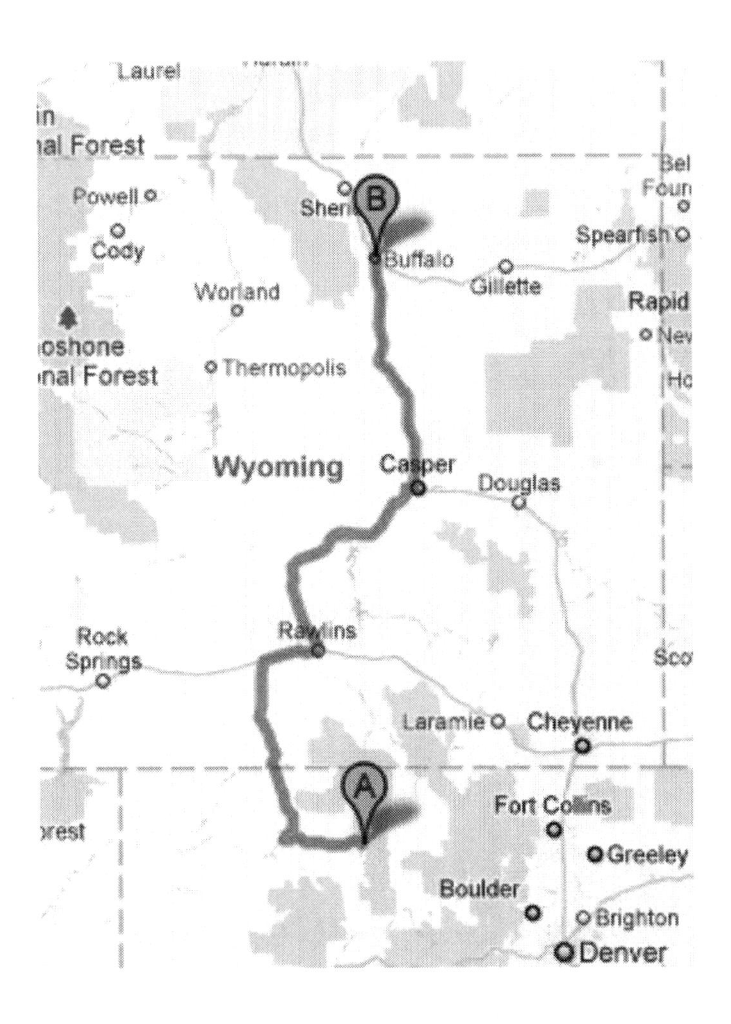

I told them in the say way they are desperate for things to do, adults are desperate for peace and quite and that is why they move to places like Buffalo, Wyoming.

All along I-70, we saw thousands of antelopes. And this was all within a hundred yards of the fence. "They are kind of a nuisance where we grew up," Wade said. "We hit them all the time."

Accidentally, of course. Everyone up there drove around with dents on the front of their cars.

Had I the chance I would have bet -- and lost -- everything I had that no way in the world would I soon find myself in Northern Nevada, running with herds of wild horses; searching for, stalking, hunting and killing antelopes. Poaching.

If the guys in those parts are eager to escape the ennui of their life on the plains, so are the girls. And their first choice is going after guys that are 5 years older, starting when they are 13. Both my companions and many of their friends found themselves on the wrong side of a sheriff's desk answering questions about their romantic escapades with young girls.

Sometimes they did it. Other times they did not. Telling your parents about imaginary romantic encounters with the local ill-shaven hoods is also a popular pastime on the plains.

Soon we were in Buffalo, and armed with complete instructions as to where to eat and how not to mention their names because some people knew they were troublemakers, we parted as friends. This is when I started to take picture of my rides.

And yes, people at the diner did know who they were, and after giving me the fish eye for even knowing these guys, they were happy to hear my two new buddies were shaping up with good jobs and new cars.

History occurs twice, said Marx: Once as tragedy. Once as comedy. These two budding newly mannered gentlemen were about a year from entering the comic phase of their adolescence.

These small towns are intoxicating. The two young guys felt trapped in Buffalo but I felt as if I could stay a few weeks. But no: I had places to go. So the next morning I was on my way to Mt. Rushmore. Still a ways off.

How far I do not know or care. I'm a wanderer, not a dag gone mileage keeper.

I've been on the road for a few days and this is already a leisurely trip. Wake up. Lounge around. Eat breakfast. Read. Whatever.

So it wasn't until noon or so that I was out on the Wyoming freeway with my thumb out. I was still in the "I could just as easily not do this as do this' stage.

If you look at the map, the area around Buffalo had lots of squiggly lines that, a la Zen and the Art of Motorcycle Maintenance, would get me to and from lots of interesting places while staying off the freeways.

But not that day. There were no side roads. At least none with even one car on them. So I walked out on the freeway and confronted what I considered to be my first road emergency. I forgot to soak my scalp in Rogaine, which is what people do when they get tired of feeling powerless about their hair falling out.

So I reached into my pack and pulled out my jar of hair grower and took care of business. Right on the highway.

Except for two horses, no one saw me. But for the rest of the trip, doing something inconvenient was my go-to move to get a ride. Anytime I was not ready, someone would stop.

I stewed beneath the big Wyoming sky for near two hours. Thank god for Ipod.

During one 30-minute stretch, not one car or truck passed. This was an interstate highway in the middle of the day, people. The main roads are the side roads out there.

It made me remember all the times in public and private places I heard people complain that Southern California or wherever had too many people living too close together.

Hey, if that is your problem, I have solution: Wyoming and South Dakota. They have more antelopes up there than people. So go. A word of warning: These don't much care for carping Californians. Or nattering New Yorkers who can't find a decent bagel. But if you can see the value in how they live, they'll like you just fine.

TONY CURTIS HAS SOME FUN

Soon a pickup leading a caravan of other pickups pulled over. I thought it was some kind of Carnie deal and I was not that far off. The driver -- Tony Curtis and his miniature greyhound puppy Dixie -- were in the front. Soon so was I -- with Dixie immediately on my lap.

"I just bought a Quonset hut on eBay in Buffalo," he told me. "170 feet long. I'm going to use 90 feet in my backyard, and sell the rest to my buddy in Georgia."

To get it home took three trips, each 200 miles, one way. Damn.

Who the hell does that kind of thing?

The answer, Tony Curtis and his dog. And his buddies. And they do it for fun. That and more. Welcome to the Midwest.

Soon an ambulance ripped past us. Tony gave him some kind of hand signal as if he knew the driver. He did. Tony owned the ambulance. He bought it when he was looking for a spare set of tires and the tires just happened to be attached to the ambulance. So he bought the whole thing. Now he was using the ambulance to transport part of his Quonset hut back to South Dakota.

The ambulance also helped him avoid the weigh stations where state inspectors sometimes inspect your cargo. I had no idea why that would be a problem and I did not ask.

I was a guest. And my job, said Tony, was making sure he did not fall asleep.

So we talked. The Quonset hut was for his Harleys, naturally. And he was going to spend the summer with his homeboys building it and painting it and fixing it up. But first he would have to travel to Mexico to get the paint. That is what he and his gang did for fun.

He also bought a 100-year old, 800-pound copper belfry from a local church. They got rid of it because a hail storm put dents in it and they wanted to replace it with one made of fiber glass. Wait till the hail gets a hold of that, he said.

"I'm going to put it on top of my Quonset hut," he said. "The copper salvage alone is worth three times more than what I paid for it."

But Tony Curtis was not in the business of turning religious artifacts into salvage. That belfry was more sacred to him than to the parishioners who had just sold it.

I guess living in a small town is no guarantee you have any common sense.

Tony was in a work outfit, or so I presumed. I also presumed his work was escaping from a Tennessee chain gang where he had been sentenced to 15 years for dealing meth to the Hell's Angels, which he probably founded but left after they got too candy-ass.

I was wrong about all that, of course. Yes he did look ragged, with neck tattoos, scraggly hair, torn pants, the whole thing. And not in a rugged kind of way either.

But by the time this trip was over, I would learn that this guy was one of the smartest and most accomplished people I had ever met. And that includes having his pilot's license after his career in the Navy.

He did not, however, know how to meet Asian girls online. I had to tell him how to do that. He was grateful. Very grateful.

DEADWOOD. GOOD OL' DEADWOOD.

And I was a lot closer to Rushmore. "Hey, you going to Deadwood?" he asked a few minutes before dropping me off. "You should go to Deadwood."

I had never heard of Deadwood the town. Deadwood the TV show? Yes. A show I never watched or wanted to watch. The town? No.

It was right on the way to Rushmore so I'd wave on my way through.

BUFFALO TO DEADWOOD.

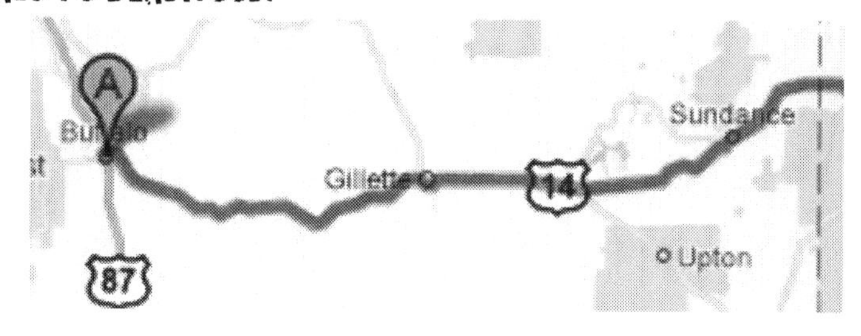

Three days later I still did not want to leave Deadwood. I had thought it was an isolated single casino sprouting out of the prairie. Wrong. It's a small town with a long and wild history. And a couple of dozen casinos.

So there were at least four very cool reasons to stay in Deadwood for a while: 1) Wild Bill Hickock was killed there, aces and eights and all. So was Calamity Jane.

2) The casinos are very homey. You plunk down $10 on a hand of blackjack and you get the feeling the pit boss is calling the local paper to let him know the big spenders are in town.

3) It's a pretty town, nestled in a narrow valley with tree covered hills all around.

And it seems there was lots of other stuff, too. Oh yeah, ghosts. In Deadwood, not too many people died of old age. Not back in the wild days.

And while people don't talk about it much, most of the folks who live there believe in ghosts.

I stayed at the Penny Hotel, which was right on Main Street. Not too far from where Wild Bill met his fate at the hands of some assassin.

(Oh yeah, I remembered another reason to like Deadwood, two of them: 1) Kevin Costner owns a casino there; and 2) The town elementary school is located right across the street -- and right next to -- two of the city's larger gaming establishments.)

And of course the lovely Dee, who with her boyfriend, are the proprietors of the Penny Hotel.

Back to the ghosts.

The folks who live there are used to supernatural disturbances. But the guy who checked me into the Penny Hotel was not. He was almost as new in town as I was and he was convinced his room was haunted. So much so he did not want to stay there -- even though it was free.

Of course I told Dee that having ghosts was a marketing opportunity par *excellance*. All she had to do was put me up for a few nights and give me a few pizzas and more people would learn about their ghostly establishment than she would ever dream of. She told me she would let me know the next day.

I always take delays as a 'no.' And besides, Dee did not want to do anything to stir the restless spirits.

The next day I'm on my way of town -- walking and window shopping -- when I heard someone shout "hey Colin."

Now when you are in the middle of nowhere and you don't know nobody -- I played craps with Kevin Costner once in Lake Tahoe, but I was not expecting my old craps playing buddy to be there -- it is strangely comforting to have someone call your name as if they were an old friend.

"Hey Colin, when you come back we'll put you up for a couple of nights and get you some free pizzas."

It was Dee, in her car, at the light. That was cool. I headed out. The greeting left me feeling good. On my way to Mt. Rushmore.

But first I would have to deal with three ladies, and one Buffalo killer.

DEADWOOD SAYS GOODBYE.

Outside of Deadwood, I rode with the ladies. Three in a row. That's probably a record. Wow. Things are different today. Earth Woman had dogs and a pickup and was heading for a campground. "I'll be back this way in a few hours if you need a lift," she offered.

Whoa.

Near Crazy Horse Sylvia wanted to know: "So what happened?" Thinking my car was sitting broken in some nearby ditch. And all I took a few things from it in this really tiny bag I was toting.

I broke it to her gently: “A few months ago I decided to hitchhike around the country and write a book about it." Her mom was in bad shape, her son broke his leg playing soccer the night before, and had she been going further, I’m sure I would have been brought up to speed on every catastrophe for a hundred miles around.

Soccer Mom soon turned off, and soon Buffalo Killer pulled over. Who would have guessed that South Dakota’s most prolific predator was a dog lover? But he was. A shiatsu?

Buffalo Killers on the Run.

No, that’s a massage. Let’s not go there.

Shitzu, yeah that is what it was. Named, ...oh hell, I forget. Nick?

But soon we got to jabbering. And this nineteen-year old told me about his girlfriend, his life in Custer, and how he was moving to Denver that summer.

"So what do you do out here," I asked, for what I thought was the second time.

"I kill Buffalo at the packing house. 250 a day."

I did the math. That was a lot of Buffalo. I turned. He had a haunted look about him.

"I also take them apart and clean them. Hey we are getting close to the Crazy Horse Memorial. I'll take you in. Locals get in free."

So the great Buffalo Hunter of Custer, South Dakota turned off into Crazy Horse Mountain. "There it is. Crazy Horse." And sure enough, about a mile away, the profile of an Indian that could have been pulled off a Buffalo head nickel gazed down at the flat black asphalt. Crazy Horse.

I took a picture of Aaron, the great Buffalo killer, and his dog. And we parted friends with best wishes for him to get to Denver, ASAP.

One hour later, I was talking to Steffi the Crazy Horse waitress about one of her fellow citizens from Custer now named Buffalo Killer. I took out my Iphone and showed her a picture.

"Oh, he's cute."

ONE YEAR LATER.

One year later, the newspaper reported that the owner's of Aaron's packing house filed bankruptcy, walked away, leaving tons of buffalo meat to rot in their giant warm room that used to be a refrigerator.

Chapter 3

Ever Want to Live in Deadwood?

Not in this lifetime, pardner.

I spent three days in Deadwood. It just felt that I belonged there. So I gambled, and lost a few hundred bucks. Which was huge since I only started with $4500.

I also spent a day walking about seeing if I could get a job as a bartender. I thought I could live there for a few months. It was not to be. Not even a nibble.

I'm the one on the right.

Chapter 4

Crazy, Crazy Horse.

If it suits you, why not.

I wanted to like Crazy Horse real bad. "Forget Rushmore, you gotta go to Crazy Horse," said a 7-11 clerk the day before. "That's a lot cooler."

And he told me about the 50-year old project to carve a huge statue of the Indian leader Crazy Horse. So big you could fit the four faces of Mt. Rushmore into the face of Crazy Horse.

I love buildings that are crazy big and last long after the builders. And Crazy Horse was right there. From the highway almost a mile away, you could see his profile, while below trucks loitered about doing whatever to get a mountain ready for more sculpting.

The statue is really a complex of exhibits and restaurants and such. And the first thing I did upon entering the museum was to search for a picture of Crazy Horse. I just wanted to compare his picture with his sculpture.

I found my answer in the corner, almost hidden away. There were no pictures of Crazy Horse, so the statue was a composite.

There were, however, lots of pictures of the Indian leader who in the 1930's came up with the idea of finding someone to create their version of Mt. Rushmore. Now that picture looked familiar: Roman nose. Only thicker. Piecing eyes. High cheeks.

That wasn't Crazy Horse up there, it was the chief who hired the German sculptor. Oh well.

It seemed like a cool place, even if the bus driver did not appreciate it when I drew attention to remarkable likeness between the chief and statue. They were not, by the way, related.

They are taking their time on the statue, with completion due in 45 years. Maybe by then Reagan will be on Rushmore.

Chapter 4

Yabba Dabba South Dakota

The Great Scoutmaster of all scouts leads me to a sacred place.

I passed through Crazy Horse, and still reeling from Steamboat, I had only one direction left: Down, down, down.

So I drifted for what could have been minutes, hours, days. I thought I had hit bottom. But no, bottom was still a few hours away.

All I know is that when I woke up, I was staring at a computer screen in Custer, South Dakota -- Home of the Flintstone Amusement Park.

Custer... Custer... Custer... Wait a minute: Weren't we within a stone's throw of the Crazy Horse Memorial? Mt. Rushmore? And a bunch of other natural and unnatural national attractions? Yes.

But at this hotel in this computer screen, the Flintstones got top billing. This I had to see. No, not just see: experience.

As if by magic, my eyes were drawn to the local paper, where a notice proclaimed that the Flintstone Theme Park wanted to hire costumed actors to play Fred and Barney.

If it was bigger and better than Rushmore and Crazy Horse, I knew I had to answer the call.

One phone call later, I was on my way to see a man called Greg.

I arrived early. Never pays to be late to an audition.

The park was closed but I wandered the grounds where a crew was spreading paint and concrete on the various booths. There was a Flintstones movie theater, radio station, train, dental office, you name it.

They even had a Mt. Rocksmore where Fred and Barney and Wilma and Betty were enshrined in stone.

I put aside all thoughts about having a theme park that depended on 45-year old memories of a cartoon show. Or having a business that needed your customers to have parents who liked Rosie O'Donnell.

As the Boss says: Out here there's just winners and losers, and don't get caught on the wrong side of that line.

But Rosie was nowhere to be seen. So I was safe. At least for the moment.

I got the tour. I got the stories. I got into the character. I got ready to see Greg about my debut as a Flintstone. Fred.

But it was over before it began: "Nope, too tall."

The wind blows cold in South Dakota in May. This you can believe. Even so, I was ready for my RV to whisk me to Rushmore.

Never happened. I did get to see a lot of wild buffalo roaming through a huge state park, though.

I saw the Flintstones but Rushmore would have to wait.

My boots are bothering me. I think they will just take some getting used to. Another bit of self and belated discovery: I am idiot for thinking that.

Chapter 5

My South Dakota Short Game

Just when I thought I was out. They pulled me back in.

"You a golfer?" was the first thing I said. He was driving a Cadillac and pulled over for me outside of Rapid City South Dakota.

"Yeah, I'm going to a tournament."

I'm wearing a Titleist hat and a golf shirt.

Turns out he was from Southern California -- Orange County and had lived in Escondido. The wind was blowing 30-35 miles an hour -- ALL DAY LONG. No gusts. Just wind. Welcome to the plains.

"Guess there won't be any golf today, too much wind."

And no Mt. Rushmore either. Not today. If you can't play golf in it -- and I've golfed in sleet and howling wind -- then I do not see why anyone would want to visit the four dead presidents in it either. Soon he was going about ten miles out of his way to drop me off at a truck stop in Rapid City -- which in these parts is basically Manhattan. Where I picked up the following golf related email on my good ole Iphone:

Hey good ole Colin!

So I want to thank you for getting me started with golf. I have been playing and hitting almost everyday out here. A guy worked with me the other day that worked with Harvey Penick. I thin it is crazy coincidence that you gave me the little red book and I had no idea I would be out here in his back yard. To read the book and hear him talking about course and people that are so close. I live jogging distance from Barton Creek.

I had also had no idea how great you were setting me up to learn the game the right way. Now I have great appreciation. I thought the fact that you got me a Driver,wedge and putter, (in reverse order of course) was merely coincidence. Now I know. So guess what my best clubs are to this day...driver and wedge shots.

Kia still talks about you, and she is now on the 7th grade golf team and she is always asking me to go to the driving range. But track is still her strongest for now. She is 200m champion and is undefeated. But of course the goal is UT golf!

You have to let me know if you are ever in the area (25% of all new US golf courses have been built in Austin over the last 5 years). Thanks again for the great introduction, I am forever great full (addicted, but grateful).

Sincerely,

Matthew Neel

Xceleration Sports Performance Labs

512 803 4229

http://WhyBeSlow.com

P.S. The woods are full of long hitters!

Matt was my personal trainer in Murrieta, California. The reason I joined his club was because it had a golf simulator where

Matt and I would work out. Anyway, he may not know it, but I think he just inserted himself into this little trip's itinerary.

Back to the golf: After leaving the truck stop, my first ride was from a mother and son, both golfers, going to pick up her husband at a local golf course.

Golf. Golf. Golf. I love that game. But soon it would be the last, last thing on my mind.

Chapter 6

Along Came Jordy

Forrest sings a song.

Then came Jordan. Jordy, to her friends. Of which I became one.

This was a very pretty, very petite, very friendly, and very stoned young lady.

"You want some pot?" She asked me.

People still smoked pot? Oh yes. In a few weeks, I would learn that I was about the only one on this planet who did not.

"No, I'm good," I said as I watched her load up her pipe and steer with her left thigh while we passed a big old noisy truck. "Sorry I can't help you load it but I don't know how."

I wasn't enabling. I didn't want her car to get crushed beneath the 18-wheeler.

"That's OK, I got it."

Jordy was studying to be a nurse and looked forward to the day when she could ply her skills "in Cali."

Hey, I was down with that.

"If you don't mind me asking, how old are?"

"19"

Oh jeez.

Isn't there some kind of law about 53-year old guys casting lecherous glances at 19-year old friends? Ask me if I care. Go ahead. Make my day. Besides, if there were, every college professor in America would be doing hard time.

We jabbered some more. Mostly me telling her that there were lots of cool ways to make money and lots of cool things to see out there, outside of South Dakota, if that was what she wanted. Later she would say she though she was the one talking my head off.

I confessed that the same, monotonous quality of life in the Badlands that drove so many kids her age nuts was actually a pretty cool way to get peace and quite when you get older. Like good ol' Colin.

She thought that was cool and told me: "I'm glad I gave you a ride. You give off lots of positive vibes."

I still got it. Oh yeah, I still got it. Maybe my next stop would be following the Grateful Dead on their next tour.

All too soon, what I did not have anymore was Jordy driving me around and smiling.

So with visions of sugar plums dancing in my head, I put my thumb out and began to walk. Backwards, mostly.

Sometimes I walk. Sometimes not. When you are out in the middle of nowhere (and whenever you see large, green, concrete, prehistoric creatures of any kind near the road, you know you are in the middle of nowhere), and no cars are around in any direction, and the wind is blowing very very hard -- wind tunnel hard -- and the clouds are getting darker and closer and lower, you walk.

At least until you find shelter.

HEY FORREST, WASSUP?

Today I walked. Three/four miles later the big green lizard looked life-sized and Forrest pulled over. And sure enough, soon we were jabbering. He was very impressed that I had just gotten a ride with Jordy. I was impressed that he was a truck driver at a coal mine in Wyoming, going home for the weekend. His truck tires were 12 feet high -- the kind of truck that the two other truck drivers from Buffalo would have paid to drive.

I asked him about my favorite book, Forrest Gump and whether he had read it. "Sure did," he said.

In contrast to the great movie of the same name, the book Forrest Gump featured more of the antics of Alabama cum Raider quarterback Ken Stabler. A few months before I had a chance to meet and hire Stabler. "Mr. Stabler, what did you think of that book Forrest Gump?"

"I like Winston Groom but stuff about me in there is a bunch of shit." And he said it just the way they did in the movie. Oh yeah.

Now that Forrest knew I was a Man of the Arts, we talked music. "Hey you wanna listen to one of my CD's?"

"Sure."

Forrest was a singer/songwriter, giant truck driver who made CD's for his friends of music he wrote and performed. They were pretty good. Nice harmonies. He did all the voices and instruments himself. Mostly about girls.

"I write songs about when I first meet em; when I feel in love with them; and when they screw me over," he said.

I was sure Jody would never do that. Hell, had he been hitchhiking instead of me he'd probably be married and living in Cali by now. Later I would learn they would probably choose Mendo County.

"I bet chicks love that," I observed with all the sagacity of the average old dude who has spent a lot of time watching the different ways guys get different girls while occasionally finding one landing in your own lap, bidden or not.

CUSTER TO PIERRE

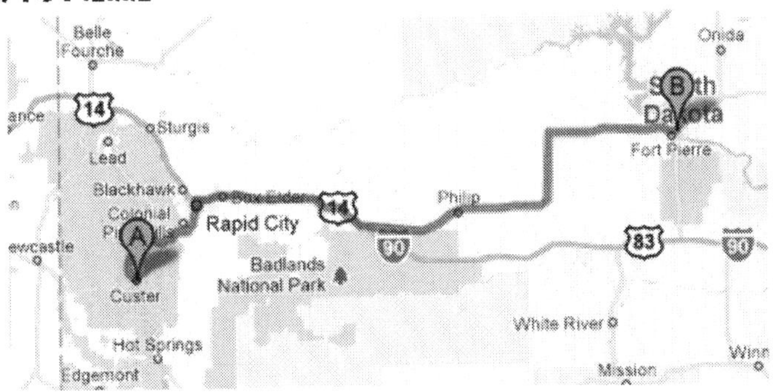

Banging a guitar is still the best way to get a girl. And if you happen to sing a bit, that closes a lot of deals that most of us never even realize are on the table.

"Yeah they do." He smiled.

But Forrest was an artist in search of a great song. Not a con man in search of a mark. Which of course is the greatest con of all, if you will pardon the cynicism.

I wanted to tell him about Steamboat Springs -- wanted to warn him away from the Enemies of Art that lurk so close to the surface, waiting to devour the unsuspecting traveller. Wanted to let him know how they treat true artists there. But I didn't.

Hitchhiking rules and all that. So 31 Miles outside of Pierre, South Dakota, I remembered that pain is no enemy of art.

Chapter 7

Pierre is a pretty nice.

Then came the first of many sympathy rides.

Rides from people who do not usually pick up hitchhikers, but who also do not care to come back and scrape their emaciated bones from the roadway three days later.

Kevin the Rancher and I talked ranching all the way into good ol' Pierre. Did you know that cows needed to be milked twice a day? Sometimes three, I found out later. My self discovery now included farm animals.

And that's how I got to Pierre, the capitol of South Dakota. But which is really pronounced 'peer' and which you would probably know if you were born a rambling sort.

Next stop Fargo?

(This is not Kevin. It is the radio repairman from International Falls who looks just like him.)

Chapter 8

Family Business in Fargo

On the road with The story of Kevin Flaherty

Once I reached Rushmore, I would be near Berlin Nelson in North Dakota, so why not see if he was up for a visit?

Berlin was a soldier in Vietnam with my brother Kevin. He was with him the night he died there.

Kev's buddies had a reunion several years ago and I met many of them and even made a video of it. But Berlin was not there. But after seeing what he wrote about Kev on the virtual Vietnam Memorial Wall

I thought I'd check him out.

So here's what he said, and what another guy said about the worst night of my life.

Berlin Nelson

Sergeant in 2LT Flaherty's Platoon

Fargo, ND., 58102, USA

Proud to Serve, With This Soldier

Kevin Flaherty was a good person, great soldier, leader, and a good friend. His loss, was felt very deep, in the hearts of the members, of the 3rd platoon.

We all, loved the guy. I keep a photo, of Kevin and the platoon, on my wall, to remind me, of my good friends and good

Americans, who served, their country, when called.

Kevin's family, can be, very proud of him. All the fellows of the 3rd, Herd, wish him smooth sailing, through the heavens. Kevin will, always have a special place, in my heart.

Sergeant Nelson.

A Letter from One of Kev's Buddies: Jack Godfrey.

Dear Sir:

My name is Jack Godfrey and I am writing to share with you my relationship with your son Kevin during our time in Viet Nam.
I have just returned from our company's Viet Nam reunion at Branson Missouri

where I had the opportunity to meet your youngest son John.

It was a very meaningful time for us all but the best and most meaningful experience for me was the time I got to spend with your son. To be able to share with him and your family the time I spent with Kevin while in the States, as well as over seas, was well enough alone worth the trip to the reunion.

I was transferred to Ft. Hood in November of 1966 after starting my basic training at Ft Lewis Washington. I was two weeks into basic when I was transferred to Texas. I had the privilege of starting basic all over again, as part of the 2nd Armored Division at Ft. Hood.

The 2nd Armored Div. was General George Patten's beloved armored division, both during World War II and after. I completed my basic and AIT training and was in the regular Army for about two months when the 198th Brigade was re-activated. I was then transferred to Bravo Company, 1st of the 52nd, where Lt. Flaherty was the 3rd Platoon leader.

Shortly after my arrival to the Third, I became Lt. Flaherty's RTO and remained that until he left us. I felt from the very first he was without a doubt the best platoon leader in the Company. I quickly recognized that Captain Goldman felt the same.

As the platoon RTO, I was always with Kevin. My responsibilities dealt with communication and supply distribution between the command level and throughout the 3rd Platoon and with each squad leader. Because of this, Kevin and I became very close, as was also the case with his replacement later on.

When I got shot, my actual condition and what had occurred, was never shared with the Platoon or the guys I left behind. I was with Kevin at the time he left us, and after talking with your son at the reunion, I wanted to personally write you and share with you what took place on that night.

For some time I have felt Kevin gave his life for the others but also he saved mine. Because of his commitment to his men and his action, he is in Heaven with our Creator, as the Bible tells us. xxxxx

The company was just south of Chu Lie at a field location called Doc Fu. Doc Fu is located just in land of a peninsula off the Ocean. Lt. Flaherty, two squads and I left base camp about 18 hundred hours that evening. Our mission was to move out about four clicks and set up an observation post. It was more of a scouting mission than anything else.

We had only moved about one click when our base camp perimeter opened fire on us.

Nothing came close, but the time it took them to understand we were under friendly fire, it had altered our operation.

After getting that action under control, we proceeded with our mission. Kevin moved out first and I quickly followed with the other squads right behind. I remember thinking at the time this was not what should happen, with Kevin out front first. I felt with the disruption of friendly fire, Kevin quickly moved out to regain the time lost, to our destined position for the night.

When I asked Kevin about our move, he responded with, "we need to get to our position."

By this time it was dark - and in Viet Nam when it is dark, it is very, very dark, pitch black. After marching another click, we came upon a river crossing. By this time, Kevin and the team had established our normal spacing for the march, which placed each man at about 10 yards from each other.

We had moved to an existing path to regain our time and this path lead directly to what had been a concrete bridge. The bridge had been bombed and the only thing that remained was the structure on each bank bridge as debris in the river.

Kevin had already reached the river and some how crossed with out interruption, he was climbing out on the other side when I started into the water. I had only moved a couple of yards into the water when I hit the first piece of concrete debris.

When the concrete edge hit my chin, I stopped with some pain and moved a little to the right.

I then ran into another, which moved me again farther to the right and around the bridge buttress where I finally could move straight through to the other side. When I reached the other side and climbed out Wiggins was close behind me, who was followed by Seus just starting across, Seus also carried a radio as a forward observer for our artillery support unit back at Battalion base camp.

The remainder of the team followed. I later thought the delay caused by the friendly fire, put us at the river crossing about the time the ocean tide was changing and receding.

As we started to cross the tide change continued to cause the river current flow to the ocean to increase dramatically moving us further to the right as were crossing.

Kevin and I had moved about 30 yards further when I first heard the Seus had unknowingly stepped off the edge of a large hole, and was in trouble.

We later found whole to be there because of the sharp bend in the river. As I returned to the edge of the river, Wiggins had already removed his gear and jumped back in the water to help Seuis. I had removed my radio and extra ammo and was going the river's edge, when Kevin grabbed my shoulder and said, "you stay with radio - I will go".

He then dropped his rifle and extra gear and entered the water. It was so dark that we could see nothing, but could hear the sound of the men struggling in the river. By this time the current was at its peak, flowing to the Ocean.

In the darkness, no one knew which way to go and I am sure each of them felt he had to go back the way they went in making there struggle even greater. After I reached base camp and could coordinate flares to mark and light our position, we then could see that had they let the current just carry them along, they were only a short distance from the bank at the bend of the river. I was the last man to see your son.

He had saved my life that night by going out there himself and ordering me to stay on the riverbank. It was a very long night and all three members that went down were a great loss to each of us in the platoon.

During my time with Kevin, both before going to Viet Nam and our time there, that was the kind of man he was.

He was very respected by everyone in our platoon and the company. He was there for each of us as well as his command. For me the reunion was very rewarding in several ways but I felt the greatest part was to meet Kevin's brother and to be able to tell him about my time shared with Kevin.

To share with him not only his loss and your loss, but also what a loss it was for me as well. Although I was later wounded and would have to come home to recover, I always remembered how Kevin gave his life that night for others.

He definitely gave me mine. I hope this will give you some peace knowing what had taken place for Kevin on that night. It is a part of Kevin that showed his quality and values, values he placed on human life and the lives, the quality leader he was. I thank you for the time-shared with your son and

I share in your loss. I apologize to you for not finding you and sharing with you earlier. Sincerely, Jack Godfrey RTO - LT. Kevin Flaherty

Thursday, August 28, 2003

I will see Berlin in a day or so.

A Letter from Tom Maloney

Monday Veteran's Day 19

To the Flaherty Family

One cold fall Friday night in 1968 when I
was running for City Council, I was going door to door
on your side of 26th St. I remember knocking on
your door to ask for support. As I walked away
I thought of Kevin, remembering him at C.O.K and
playing basketball with him at "the Yard". At th
moment I realized how lucky I was to be able
seek public office and sensed a feeling of gui
that Kevin was less fortunate. My eyes fi
I stoped knocking on doors and went home.
was a very personal moment, the kind that
very difficult to share but a moment I often rem

Last Saturday I was in Washington with
three year old son Christopher and a friend. W
stoped at the Vietnam Veterans Memorial. Th
was a church-like reverence as thousands of people
passed by the Memorial. It was a reverance I hav
experienced at memorials in Leningrad and Sov
but never before in my own country. I loo
on "the Wall" for Kevin's name but I co
not find him because there were so many n
but I wanted you to know that he is still rem
and his sacrifice will always be appreciated

Sincerely

Tom Maloney

Chapter 9

Getch Yer Free Food in Pierre

Current mood: blustery

"Do you want some food?"

I looked around. The 20-something young lady was talking to me. That happens a lot in the Midwest. You go into a store and hear the clerk say hello to an old friend. Only he is talking to you.

You get into an elevator and some stranger says in a cheerful voice: "What floor would you like?"

So you have to be ready. This day I was not.

I was standing on a corner outside of Pierre, South Dakota, watching the world go by as I made my way to Fargo.

I did not feel hungry. Though someone offering me food usually makes me so.

Nor did I look distressed. Or so I thought before this young lady parked her late model car a few feet away and, leaving her companion, walked towards me with both arms outstretched. One holding a bottle of Evian. The other a can of Pringles.

Pringles?

Maybe it was some kind of secret hobo food. Less than one hour before I had just finished the part of Atlas Shrugged where Ayn Rand declared altruism the greatest crime of the 20th century. I guess that made this generous young lady a criminal.

I'd have to figure it all out. Though I was pretty sure that hitchhikers were a part of the Randian universe. (She did make a hitchhiker/hobo the vice president of her company.)

I put off dialing 911. Of course, I still had a phone then. And a computer.

"That's OK. I have some water and I just ate. But thank you. Thanks a lot."

"You sure?"

"Yeah, but thanks."

She walked away, disappointed. I should have accepted the water and fried rice chips with gratitude. But I was flat footed.

After surviving this brush with pure evil, I wished I had the presence of mind to ask to take her picture. If not for my book, for the FBI's Ten Most Wanted List.

She and her accomplice made their escape. And I was on the road again.

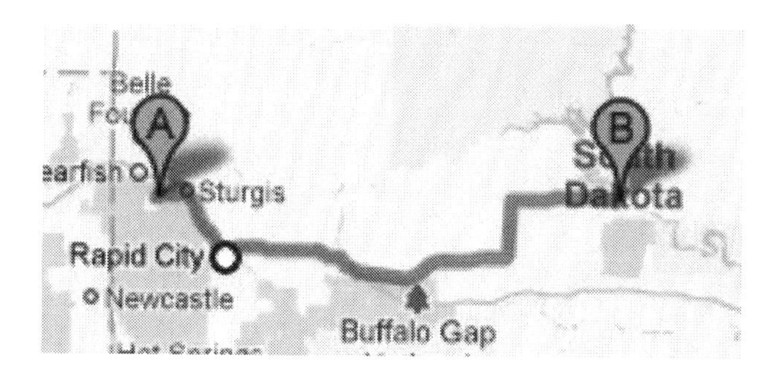

Even before the Pierre Welcome Wagon arrived with Meals on Wheels, I could not help but notice how folks in these parts were so friendly. They wave as they go by with minivans full of kids. They smile. They point to where they are turning off as if it is somehow impolite for them to be unable to give a complete stranger -- apparently a poor hungry stranger at that -- a ride for a few hundred miles in the direction of his choice.

Nice folks.

I've also been getting a lot of dog rides. And for some reason I remember the dog's names more than the owners.

Fifteen minutes after Paula Pringle drove away, Missy and her big-fisted rancher owner were pulling over in a pickup truck.

"I've already passed you by twice, guess I better take you where you can get a lift."

That was fine by me so that is what he did while Missy the French Poodle with a spiked metal collar sat on my lap. I looked around for the Pringles. No such luck.

"Nobody will bother you here, but just across the county line, the state troopers will pick you up and take you across the county. They'll phone ahead to the next county where the state troopers will take you across it as well."

Great. A relay race. I had visions of riding in speed and comfort police cruiser style all across America. Maybe I'd finally get some Pringles. But no such luck. I thought he was just kidding and so was I.

That's crazy. Who ever heard of cops giving rides to hitchhikers. I was wrong. Again. As I would find out many times.

After Missy and her owner dropped me off, all I had was a guy who took me 300 miles to the Lone Steer Hotel in Steele, North Dakota; passing through, fortuitously enough, the birthplace of Lawrence Welk, and home to a few museums to remember him by.

He was from Denver and on his way home through the rolling, rocky and tree-lined hills of North Dakota to visit Mom for Mother's Day. Damn, this hitchhiking thing was easy: Just stick out your thumb and someone who knows all about the countryside will pick you up, give you a tour, then drop you off at a cheap and clean motel right on the highway. Where you can catch an NBA playoff game.

The Lone Steer hotel looked simple enough: Just a hotel and a restaurant with the obligatory statue of a very big and very green prehistoric animal standing out from the prairie.

My hotel room was dark. Very and oddly dark. Which was nice. But I still wanted to taste some North Dakota prairie flavor so I opened the curtains.

This was a first: My window opened directly onto a large ballroom dance floor. Also kind of dark -- and unoccupied -- except for a small string of white Christmas lights. It looked as if it had once been a courtyard that now had a roof. And was just a few hours away from the local Christmas party.

Next day at breakfast, it all made sense: "That's where they hold the bull auctions." The food was not free.

Give my regards to Lawrence.

Chapter 10
On the Way to Fargo
The good Lord told him to turn around and pick up good (ol') Colin

After leaving Bull Auctions and Big Birds behind in Steele, North Dakota, I set out for Fargo.

Thirty minutes later I squeezed into Jonathan's car. We jabbered about his career as a motocross rider, an engineer, and now, the spreader of the word of the Lord.

"When I drove by you the Lord told me to turn around and pick you up," he said.

And here I had been praying for a luxury RV full of Asian girls.

"The lord works in mysterious ways his wonders to perform," I reminded him, saying that perhaps he was not sent back to convert me, but perhaps the Lord had a reason to get me to Fargo in a hurry. Or to delay his arrival in Minnesota, where he was a mechanical engineer for a company that makes exercise machines.

Or maybe there was an RV of Asian girls on the way to pick me up and the Lord decided for reasons of his own that I should not be in their company. I thought it over like one of those religious conundrums with no answer but the contemplation of it was supposed to bring enlightenment.

Hey, it was working.

I know the Bible lingo. That's 12 years of Catholic School kicking in. Over the next two months, at least ten other drivers would turn their car around and come back for me -- for reasons known only to them and their maker. But I did wonder if divine intervention was somehow keeping me from my Asian RV destiny.

I may not have shared any of my religious musings with Jonathan, who looked like your average North Dakota guy. Just for fun, the day before, he and his Dad jacked up his car, took off the wheels, slid out the axle, did something to it, then put it all back together. With no parts left over!

It probably did not occur to them that it was fun. But if you enjoy what you do, that is what fun is.

And that car was running smoo-ooth.

Anyway, for the next 160 miles, I gently and politely fended off his attempts to turn me to the Lord. I knew in my heart of hears that if the good Lord had any conversion plans for me, it would involve an RV full of you know what.

I would have signed up for that in a heart beat. But as I must tell you for the 874 time, that did not happen.

I did, however, promise I would read one proverb a day for 30 days. I'll keep you posted. (Jeez, I thought a proverb was a few lines long. Like something you can fit on a bumper sticker. Heck: Each one is a couple of pages. I got hosed. But I survived.)

He was a great kid and we parted friends. Though he was disappointed when I told him that a lot of Christians had tried to get me off the bench, but that was where I was staying as far as getting all religious games were concerned. Until the RV arrived, I remembered.

A few minutes later I was in my hotel reading a poster about a traveling Vietnam War memorial that was in Fargo for two weeks, starting today. Is that what they call Kismet?

I have now turned into one of those people who doesn't mind tossing around vague religious terms if it will make him look cool.

I called Berlin, one of the guys who was with my brother when he died in Vietnam. That's why I was in Fargo.

It was Mother's day.

"Hey Berlin, I'm sorry I forgot it was mother's day. And although I took a few months off, I guess I just forgot that civilization will rumble on without me even when I am gone. So we do not have to meet today if you have other obligations."

We arranged to meet the next day.

HOW TO OVER-PREPARE FOR AN ADVENTURE.

It is easy to over prepare for a hitchhiking trip. Almost any preparation could be too much. But by now I was starting to figure out that I had not figured on having such bad shoes. Boots.

I was not a boot person. I owned two pair and enjoyed wearing them once every three or four months. But that was it.

Two years ago, at the end of my favorite show, 24, the hero Jack Bauer walked off into the sunset wearing a pair of cowboy boots.

Cool, I thought. Very cool. Now there was a dude who had his act together: Saving civilization in cowboy boots.

So when it came time to shoe up for this trip, I cast aside a pair of hiking boots in favor of my cool cowboy boots.

Only when it was too late for me to do anything about it did I learn these boots are made for riding horses. Not walking.

But walk I did. And by the end of every day, my lower legs and toes felt cramped and sore. But they did look good. Now I knew another reason why chicks are pissed off so often at guys: It's the legs.

Chapter 11

Doin' it for themselves in the Dakotas

The brothers and sisters and doing it for themselves.

Self reliance means spending less $50 a day in a restaurant. The folks in the Badlands do it a bit differently.

Everybody does everything.

So I get a ride from another rancher outside Pierre.

"Seems like everyone up here is everything all at the same time," I said. "Carpenter, mechanic, plumber, you name it."

"Well yesterday I was up doing some roofing, and a few weeks ago during calving season, I had to do a Cesarean section on a cow."

Cow C-Sections? Who knew. Not this city kid. But I had been watching the local farmer cable TV. So I asked about DNA.

"Oh yeah, we do DNA testing and select for at least ten traits on ten different genes. Ten years ago a seven month old calf might weigh 380 pounds. Now they weigh 600 and more. Then we send them to the finish lots."

The places that drive city slickers with new homes crazy with weird smells for miles around.

Miles Before Wal-Mart.

Mark offered me a beer. “No thanks.” For some people, alcohol is an addiction. For others, a habit and I just fell out of mine a long time ago.

Mark No-Wal-Mart had five kids and took me way out of his way. "If I want to go to Wal-Mart, that's 120 miles away. Plumbers and stuff won't come out here. Too far. Too expensive anyway. So we do it ourselves."

The Flintstones finally made sense. When I think of that cartoon show I think Fred and Barney tooling around Bedrock in a car made of wood with stone wheels and feet for brakes.

I swear I expect somebody to pick me up in a car they made themselves -- probably of timber and antlers.

Mark No-Wal-Mart's wife was out that day helping her brother with his 4000 cattle. Vaccinating and castrating.

Gulp.

If these folks want a burger, they go kill it. A salad, they grow it. A better car, they fix it.

These are some hard working, hardy people.

A few months later a literary agent would scoff at the idea that there was anything interesting to see anywhere in America. It's all Wal-Marts, strip malls, freeways, and crap.

That's what it looks like from Manhattan, for sure.

I told him about Mark.

He said "Sorry. I didn't know."

CATTLE RUSTLING ON THE PLAINS.

I'm back with a Rancher. Apparently there is more than one in these parts.

We drive into a small South Dakota town with a gothic looking bridge rusting over the water. "We used to swim in that," said the rancher. "After the football games. No more though."

"What about cattle rustling? " I ask as innocently as possible for someone contemplating a new career in bovine thievery.

"Don't see much of it out here."

But the cattle don't get branded for a few months. "So how do you know if anyone is stealing them?" I asked. "Do you count?"

He smiled at the prospect of the cowboy-booted Last Poet trying to make off with a cow, any cow. Not just his. Ridiculous. "No. But the people in the packing houses know all the ranchers so even if someone stole some, they would have no where to take them."

"Dang," said the Last Poet. "Thus endeth my career as a cattle rustler, even before it begins."

I silently cursed Larry McMurtry for planting these felonious visions in my over-heated poetic brain.

Soon I was in my hotel room, checking out the NBA playoffs.

For all the time I spent playing basketball as a kid – and that pretty much means all the time – I have not watched an entire NBA game on TV or anywhere else for decades.

Now I'm catching a few a week. It makes me feel tethered.

PIERRE TO TEPPEN

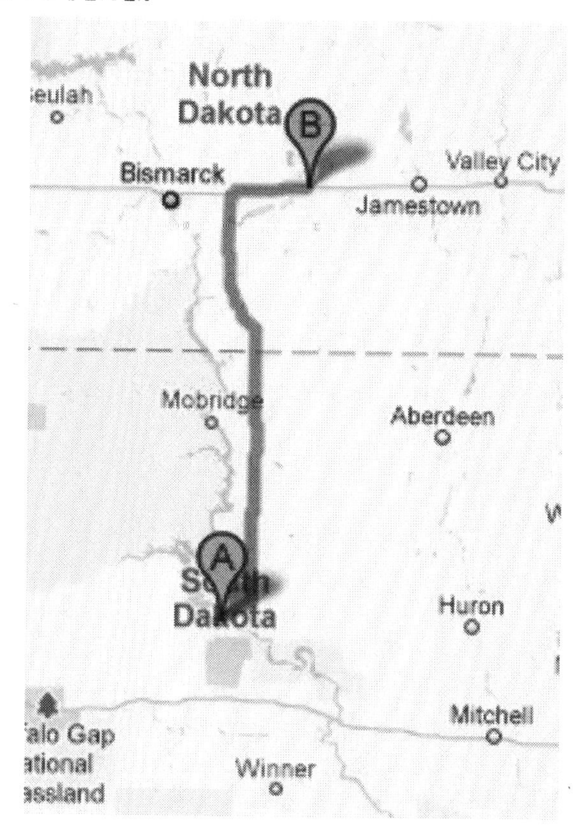

Chapter 12

Meeting in Fargo

Ever since I was 12 years old, I've always known I would meet Berlin Nelson.

At the time I did not know his name. But I always knew that someday I would go find the people who were with my brother when he died in Vietnam.

My brother Kevin and I were close. He called me Coles. We shared a queen sized bed for five years. Sometimes I would act as a go between with another kid my age who had a sister Kev's age. "My brother likes your sister Sheila," I told Johnny Pankowski. Though to this day he does not remember this.

When Kev left for the Army, I got up early and, with my Dad, drove to the armory where he reported for duty. The next summer, my mom suggested that maybe I should stay home from two weeks at Boy Scout camp so I could spend time with Kev before he shipped out to Southeast Asia.

(I don't even like saying the name of that country.)

I did not have the slightest idea what she was talking about.

But I did watch through a gauzy porch window as he packed the family station wagon and headed off to the airport with our dad.

A few months later I looked through that same window to see two guys in Army uniforms standing on our front steps and asking if my parents were around.

I did not have the slightest idea what they were doing there.

But I soon found out Kev was missing. And it never occurred to me even for one second that he was anything but missing. Missing things are found. No big deal. My brother, after all, spent a week at jungle survival skill in Panama eating snakes that tasted like chicken.

My brother Dave has the exact same memory. Except he is the one answering the door.

I cried at school at the oddest moments. Joey Bucci told me Kev was in the jungle with the guerillas swinging from the trees. Then hopped around making ape noises. I started laughing real hard. Then started crying for the first time.

A few days later I opened the same front door to see the same guys wearing the same uniform. I called my folks.

Pat Ritchie called on the phone and asked how things were going. I said they found Kev.

"Alive?"

"No."

I was 12.

A few days later, I received a few letters back that I had written him. Deceased. Return to sender. My mom used to send him Brownies every week. I don't know if any came back. Nor do I remember if she ever made brownies for us again. She could have done so three times a day for three years and I still would not remember.

I don't remember anything for that whole period except the girls were friendlier and the teachers were more tolerant. And spending a lot of time at Pat's house, playing basketball, surrounded by many of his nine brothers and sisters and widowed mom.

Kev's death was a nuclear holocaust that blew our family apart. And as I told Berlin Nelson in a Fargo coffee shop just a few hours ago, I have thought of Kev every day since then.

But I rarely spoke of him. My mom took it the worst. She turned our house in a mini-museum of Kev, his boots in the living room and his army pictures and momentos all around.

They went to his grave every Sunday after Church.

When they asked me if I wanted to go, I always said no. After a while they stopped asking. I've only been there once. I was forced. Don't ask.

The first time I took my then-wife to visit Wilmington, she started asking about my brothers and sisters and what they were doing and where they were.

"So where is your brother Kevin?" she asked.

"He's dead."

"You always talked about him as if he were alive."

Yeah.

A few years ago, my friend Craig broached the unbroachable with me and asked about Kev in a curious fashion: "He committed suicide, didn't he?"

"What the fuck are you talking about you stupid shit. He was a hero. He died trying to save the lives of his men."

"Sorry, I didn't know."

And that was that.

An old girlfriend read an earlier portion of this blog and she too was surprised to learn that my brother died in Vietnam.

I didn't keep it a secret. I just kept it private because it was so precious to me. My friends in San Diego who knew, Jack and Mick, visited the memorial when they went to Washington D.C. and brought back a rubbing for me.

I said thanks and that was that.

A few years ago, Kev's buddies started having reunions. The Third Herd they called themselves. Maybe that's why my brother always told them to 'saddle up.'

I went to one in the middle of nowhere Missouri. Berlin missed that one. He went to the next ones that I missed.

I don't know why or how, but just the fact that Kev's friends from the Army still remember him is important to me. An enormous comfort to me. And I know it is to Kev's friends in Wilmington as well.

Berlin is a big shot college professor in Fargo, North Dakota. He has four children and a wife from Costa Rica.

We had coffee at the local bistro and talked about families and homes and friends before touching gently on his old friend Kev.

"I still have his photograph on the wall in my home," Berlin told me. "I've told my wife and kids about him many times."

And when his son called, all Berlin said was that he was having coffee with Kevin's brother.

Berlin described Kev as other soldiers in Kevin's platoon did. Gregarious. Open. Liked. Respected.

Berlin was a sergeant, one of four in Kev's platoon. They trained together and knew each other for a good part of their time in the army. Kev was not there very long before he died after jumping into a turbulent river at night to rescue several members of his squad who were having trouble crossing.

I knew all that.

I'm not sure Berlin knew what I was doing there. What I wanted to know.

Chapter 13

Uncle Eddy and the Departure

May 13, 2009 - Wednesday

Berlin did not want to let me go. We had just finished having lunch with his son, who had heard about Kev and seen pictures of him all his life.

And Berlin was taking me to the road North.

He was hemming and hawing, as if some other way besides hitchhiking would present itself before he dropped me off. I tried to make him feel better by telling him about the one year I spent traveling the southeast flying First Class and staying in nice hotels.

So this was an interesting change of pace.

His reluctance reminded me of my Uncle Eddy when he was dropping me off at the freeway in 1976. Which I told Berlin, since it involved Kev.

I was hitchhiking my way out West, and I stopped to visit Uncle Eddy in Northern Virginia. Uncle Eddy was a spy. For our side. At least that is what I always believed, even now.

He was born in Japan to American missionaries so he was fluent in the language.

He did a lot of banking in China during the 30's – he was one of the last American's to leave Shanghai before the war.

During the war he interrogated Japanese prisoners, and went into Nagasaki with MacArthur soon after the blast.

After the war, Uncle Eddy "traded tobacco" throughout Asia, meeting the top leaders in Phillipines, Vietnam and other countries in the region. I always thought that was a cover story.

I visited him a few times and asked him about it more than a few times. Whatever he said, I always paid more attention to the twinkle in his eye during my interrogation than to what he was saying.

Kev was one of the great regrets of Uncle Eddy's life.

"I told your brother I wanted to call Theiu before he left, but he said not to," Uncle Eddy told me for the tenth time as we neared my drop off. "I wished I had." Not that anything would have changed, but Uncle Eddy felt somehow it would have.

Uncle Eddy later told me he thought I was going to be out there hitchhiking for weeks before I got a ride. But he drove by 20 minutes later and I was gone.

That's what I told Berlin before getting out of the car.

So out I went, and within 45 minutes I would accomplish one of my major goals for the entire trip.

Chapter 14

Why You Pushin' Me.

Finally.

"Why you pushin' me?" I said with a flat voice from the back seat of the police cruiser.

Berlin had just dropped me off on a small road headed to Canada, just over the river from Fargo in Minnesota.

A state police cruiser pulled over, and as if from central casting, an officer got out.

"Got any weapons or drugs I should know about?"

"No."

"Mind if I check?"

"Go ahead."

I offered him my pack and put out my arms. He frisked me.

"Got any ID?"

Ten minutes later, I was in sitting on a hard, plastic seat much like you would find in a booth at McDonald's. In front of me was a screen. Not a TV screen, a 'keep the criminal in place' screen. At my feet a drain. This was clearly the kind of place that needed to be hosed down every so often. The back of a police car.

"... why you pushin' me?" I asked.

He smiled.

Now from the very first hour of this trip, I knew I would have to get into some trouble or at least interesting spots if I were going to make this book interesting to anyone more than genealogists 100 years from now.

So I said ..."why you pushin' me," just like I told Tim I had wanted to do on my very first ride out of Colorado to Steamboat Springs.

It is of course a quote from the first Rambo moved called "First Blood." As in "he drew first blood."

I knew that during this trip I would have to say this to a cop to make my trip complete.

And I just had. One more thing off the bucket list. All that is left is hopping a train and maybe one or two other things.

So I was happy.

I never said I would have to do it in anger. After frisking me, the cop asked if I wanted a ride north about 30 miles.

"Sure," I said.

So off we went. And of course we were jabbering. I told him about my little project and what I had found so far.

And nine minutes later I told him about my first trip and what I had told Tim about finding some cop to ask: "... why you pushin' me?"

So as far as I was concerned, that counted.

He laughed and pulled up to a gas station/soda fountain two miles from his house.

"I have to go home and take care of some business, but if you are here in 30 minutes, I'll take you farther North."

Sure. 30 minutes later, having just learned just about everything that a man can learn about trapping and cooking selling 'rats," which of course are muskrats, I was back in the cruiser heading North.

He told me instead of Canada I should check out Lake in the Woods, or Woods in the Lake, which sounded good to me. He showed me all the cop gadgets, the radar for tracking multiple cars in both directions, the radios, the computers: Pretty cool guy stuff.

Then we got into family and kids and things like that. And I put on my customary 'All Star Dad' hat – that is when I still had it, of course -- and told him a few facts of life about kids and exes and how it all is supposed to work.

There may have been an abusive step-father around his kid and he did not now what to do. So I told him.

Soon he dropped me off and I was checking my email.

One was from my son basically saying that I was an asshole. And that he was going to Afghanistan soon with the Air Force.

Shit.

Message to that cop: You had a question. Watch the movie Slingblade. That is the answer.

FARGO TO LAKE OF THE WOODS

Chapter 14
Oh Ca-na-da!

Mark Steyn is a bastard. A dirty, rotten, fraudulent Canadian bastard,

and oh, People actually try and sneak into Canada?

Mark Steyn is a bastard. A dirty, rotten Canadian bastard.

And don't I know it.

For years I have been one of those sheep reading every Steyn column; hanging on every Steyn talk show; bleating at the arrival of every Steyn pronouncement like an airborne lemming. Yes, they bleat as the wind rushes through their fur.

Thanks to Steyn, I know what that feels like.

Canada was one thing Steyn was supposed to know. After all, his parents say he was born there or at least lived there for a time. Them I will believe. Probably.

Steyn has long talked about Canada and its non-existent borders, loopy civil servants, mediocrities posing as newsmen and other facts of life there.

I never questioned why Steyn left Canada, only how he got there in the first place.

In Steynland, Canadian citizenship was granted to all who showed up, praised Allah, cursed the U.S., and asked for free stuff – which they soon received in the form of wads of pocket cash and limo rides to their new (and free) luxury flats.

I will admit it now: Under the control of the Steyn-mind, I was one of these people who made fun of Canada. It's not really a country anyway said Steyn's stooges in the popular culture at South Park. It's Shelbyville, complete with a fake Garrison Keillor.

To lamely rip off a lame show. Now that is lame.

All that changed soon after I spotted the truck full of Canadian lumber headed my way. I did not think it would stop. But I'll put my thumb out to a bus full of cloistered nuns. No one gets a free pass. (Except me.)

But he did, and I climbed way up and in. Soon Peter and I were buddies. He was delivering his load of pine logs to the mill. He had driven down from Canada and after driving along a U.S. road, he would deliver his trees to the mill and then head back.

I could not place his accent. He told me it was German via Mexico, now Canada.

His 17-year old son designed video games and wanted to go to college to do it for a living. "My wife died five years ago," he told me. "She was a writer too. Poems and short stories."

So he liked the whole idea for a book. He invited me to join him as he dropped off his cargo of logs. There was only one catch: The mill was just across the border in Canada. So the plan was I would go with him, help him unload, then we would return together to the land of the free.

That plan lasted as long as it took the Canadian border agent to send Peter's truck to holding, peer inside my mind, and detain me for interrogation. Where I met my nemesis, known then only by number.

The questions flew fast and furious like a Canadian beaver through a patch of fresh pine trees.

Have I ever written another book on hitchhiking? (She, yes she, asked that one about five times...)

What are you doing here? Repeat three times. I felt like a bottle of shampoo directions.

How much money do you have? ("Three grand, I think." She counted it. "That's right.")

Over my interrogator's shoulder hovered an official portrait of her majesty Queen Elizabeth. Whom I happen to like. She was wearing some kind of Canadian symbol which I assumed had come fresh off a sweaty jersey from the Stanley Cup-winning Canadian Maple Hawks. The last time, that is, a Canadian team actually won that Canadian trophy, which I think was in 1917. Or 1817.

I guessed that at some lonely border outpost of some English colony in Africa that same portrait would have a shrunken head.

This Queen and her equally stern civil servant appeared to be thinking what just a few moments ago I had considered the unthinkable: Someone was trying to sneak into Canada.

And that someone was good ol' Colin.

"What are you going to do in Canada?"

"Unloading the timber then leaving," quoth I.

"What kind of writer are you?"

LAKE OF THE WOODS TO INTERNATIONAL FALLS.

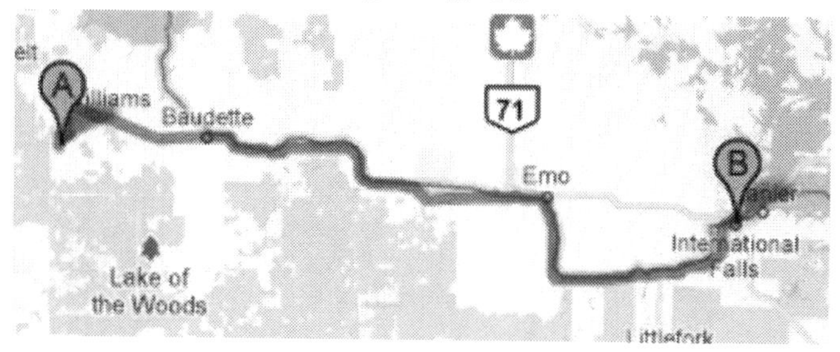

This was in my wheelhouse. I would tell her, I thought, and soon not only would she let me in, she would get me one of those big limos previously reserved for angry Muslim clerics with big beards. Probably stocked with humus and spring water. But that would be OK with me.

"Ah-he hem," I said. "My work has been published all over the world. New York Times. Wall Street Journal. LA Times. And a thousand other newspapers and magazines."

I could have gone on. I especially wanted to tell her that I should have been the Poetry Slam champ of Steamboat, but that would come later after she apologized for the holdup.

I stepped back and waited for applause. When none arrived, thought about how to continue. I did not want to close the deal with my sucker punch. She didn't care a whit. So I had no choice.

I dropped the big one on her and waited for my luxury Canadian limo to arrive.

"I'm not Mark Steyn. But I'd like to be."

That was dumb. For one thing, there is no such thing as a luxury Canadian limo. For another, she cared even less.

Now at this point, after this intense virtual Canadian waterboarding that had turned my mind upside down and soaked it in Canadian kerosene, I cannot remember if I actually said this. Or just thought it. Or why I thought mentioning this Canadian freak would be of some help.

No matter: the interrogation was over. And it was too late to take back my off-handed admiration for Steyn. I was starting to sweat. And she knew it.

"I'm denying you entry into Canada because you do not have proper ID." I waited for secret doors to open and small but tough Canadian policemen to appear.

I looked over her other shoulder at the list of things forbidden entry into Canada. I knew immediately that, in addition to leeches, lizards and snakes, Colin Flaherty would soon be on that list.

At least I was in decent company. The night before I watched part of the movie the Rock, where Sean Connery got arrested at the Canadian border trying to smuggle J. Edgar Hoover's secret files out of the country. And they put him away in a secret prison for 30 years.

My friend Paul used to be J. Edgar Hoover's room service waiter when the Big Man came to San Diego to spend a few weeks playing the ponies.

And yes, Hoover and Clyde Tolson were full blown, chiffon-gown wearing fairies. So I had a few Hoover secrets of my own that apparently did me no good at this border crossing.

She blamed it on insufficient ID, but I saw through that right away. I was bad. Bad. Real bad. And she knew it.

"In a few weeks, if you don't have a passport, you would have had trouble getting back into the states as well," she told me.

I looked at her hard. But there was nothing coming back for me -- the gringo wetback from California. No glimmer of recognition. No hint of a smile. I must have reminded her reminded her of her first ex-husband.

Meanwhile, 50 yards away and heading North at a high rate of speed was the young lady whom they had admitted right in front of me.

"All I have is a Minnesota driver's license," I heard her say. "Its my aunt's house in Minneapolis. "I had to get it so I could qualify for in-state tuition at university there. But I'm really Canadian."

Which anyone would know by the way she did not use 'the' before university.

So while my border agent and this comely looking lumberjackstress congratulated themselves on successfully organizing a conspiracy to defraud the government of the United States, I slipped involuntarily into smart ass mode.

The last defiant act of a desperate man.

"After living in San Diego for 30 years, it had never occurred to me that anyone wishing to enter the U.S. would ever have any trouble doing so," I ventured.

That was no help. No reaction. Nada. Non-Canadian meant non-person. At least until I could get me the right clerical robes.

No matter what Steyn that bastard says, these folks were serious. I replayed the interrogation in the highways and bi-ways and backstreets of my mind.

For every question they asked, they already knew the answer. I remembered all the deceptions I had tried to sneak past my inquisitor.

I had been to Canada not once but twice. I found Toronto and Winsdor to be dirty and demoralized.

How did she know?

Maybe it was the bartender in Toronto. He was working on a book about a "new theory of Canadian literature."

And yes, that was me who rolled his eyes, however briefly. I didn't mean to. Really.

Did they have some kind of crazy new Canadian thought scan-o-meter?

And what about my five year flirtation with the one of the largest criminal enterprises in the United States? True, I had given it up long ago and did not think anyone cared about my shady past anymore. But surely she had no way of knowing that I used to be a card-carrying member of the Democratic party? Did she?

This was not an interrogation any longer. Now it was sport. Catch and release the hapless Yankee.

And now this loser was on his way back to the U.S.., rejected by a country doing everything it can to protects its borders from agents of disharmony and instability.

Steyn. You bastard. Its all your fault.

In the 8 minutes it too me to cross back into the U.S., I had plenty of time to think.

They knew my deepest secrets. She saw past the facade that so successfully bedeviled her less sophisticated colleagues in law enforcement South of the border.

She knew I was dangerous. Very dangerous.

This was no toothless hound dog sitting by the fire, his best hunting seasons behind him.

Good ole Agent 16339 peered into every corner of my American soul and saw the real me: A pit bull. Vicious. Snarling. Dangerous. She knew what I was capable of. And she and Canada wanted no part of it.

I walked across the bridge head high. It was not an act. Once every secret is exposed and every dirty corner of your mind is turned inside out, and held up for inspection, there is no room left for shame.

But the eight minutes was plenty of time to cast off my old ideas about Canada as one big, fat, leech feasting off the guns and butter and treasure of its brutish neighbor to the south.

Everything Steyn said about Canada was a lie: perpetrated for his own nefarious purposes at which we should not even guess.

I had no more time to waste on that fool. With a new found respect for the iron fist guarding that treasure trove of great people and great ideas, I approached U.S. Customs with a new found humility.

My self regard alternating between flying high and rolling low, I did not even care about the prospect that I could be soon walking endlessly back and forth between the two border posts if U.S. authorities also denied me entry.

I would be a man without a home. Oops, I was already that. A man without a country, then. Without a Steyn. I deserved it. I knew that now. I did have one more card to play that guaranteed my re-entry in good standing to the good old USA:

I stumbled as if by magic the words that opened the Golden Door:

"Does anyone know the address to Michael Moore's web site?"

Great Hitchhiking Stories

When hitchhikers get together, there is usually only one story told: Who got the longest and fastest ride with the most extravagant free stuff.

A hitchhiker in Denver told me he was on his way to Montana when "a guy from Malaysia stops and takes me to his house to get breakfast. I had just woken up after sleeping at the side of the road. He told me he passed me when I was rolling up my sleeping bag and turned around to pick me up.

"Turns out they needed some help with Medicare forms. Their grandmother had just gotten out of the hospital and they needed help with Medicare and insurance forms. I helped them out., Stayed with them a week, and they bought me this bus ticket."

My father-in-law's favorite story comes from a fraternity hazing ritual at the University of Southern California. They took him up the coast, dropped him off in his underwear on the beach, and told him to find his way home.

The first house with a light was an alum of USC, who took daddy-in-law back to school, beating his tormentors by 30 minutes.

Here is mine. It comes from my friend Gary when he was in his early 20's.

My Favorite Hitchhiking/Car Stealing Story

Kiser starred in one of my top ten sports memories when he served up a fastball right in my wheelhouse in the third year of Little League. So we interrupt his great hitchhiking saga for this baseball story.

But First Some Little League

After two and half years in Little League, I did not have a single hit. So Kiser was not worried when I came to bat with the bases were loaded. The outfielders moved up. Kiser pitched. I swung and hit fence.

The rest happened in slow motion. Not because of some crazy extra sensory thing that happens during times of great athletic achievement. But because I was running very, very slowly. Which was as fast as I could.

By the time the outfielder tracked down the ball and threw it into the infield, I was rounding second and heading for third. If anyone was saying anything like, "slide, slide slide" I did not hear them; all the blood having drained from all the non-essential parts of my body, like ears, about two bases ago.

So for the first and only time in my entire and short lived baseball career I slid, kicking up what seemed to be a tornado of dust. When I emerged, safe, through the cloud of dirt, I saw something I had never seen at a Little League game before. My dad and my brother, standing at the third base fence, smiling and clapping and basking. They were proud. Two weeks later, Kev was heading west across the Pacific on a big boat with Berlin Nelson.

Back to Gary:

"I had only been in the car for a few minutes when this gay guy propositioned me. I said sure. But was it O.K. if I drove?""He said 'fine.'"

"So as he got out and walked around the car, I slid over to the driver's seat, popped the locks, and drove away."

Chapter 15

Hail Canada.

Reveling in my new status as an international outlaw – albeit a newly enlightened one – I said goodbye to my new friends at the U.S. Border and hit the road. Soon the rain began.

Finally my friends would get an answer to their most popular question: "What are you going to do if it rains?"

I looked around for some bushes or big pipes, just in case, and set the chrono on my Timex Ironman. Six minutes and 44 seconds later we had an answer to whether hitchhiking was easier in the rain.

Yes.

"Get in. It's too wet out there to walk."

Six weeks later, a crack addict would enlighten me about when people do – and do not – give you a ride in the rain. And he would be right.

Bob was a driving a panel truck that belonged to a local utility company. He drove up and down the Northern version of the Rio Grande, keeping an eye on pipes and gauges on both sides of the border.

After about 30 minutes, I kind of broke my rule about bringing potentially depressing information into the car. I broached the subject of Canadian border guards, and how some woman with blonde hair and (what I hoped was) a bullet proof vest just kicked me out of Maple Land.

"That's Judy. She's a bitch."

Judy. Badge Number 66339 now had a name.

Bob had been crossing the same bridge every day sometimes twice a day for several years. He gave me chapter and verse of several ordinary encounters that Judy turned into international incidents.

Soon we put Judy behind us as we headed toward International Falls in the rain. "I'll get you part of way there."

He pointed to the river on our left.

"Anyone can cross that river anytime they want," he said, looking at me and smiling. "I do it all the time. All you have to do is go down and ask anyone with a boat. Sometimes you can walk."

Officially, Minnesota is known as the Gopher State, mostly to outsiders. But mostly it is the Walleye State, especially this time of the year when fishing is the chief topic of conversation in these parts.

That morning the front page of the local papers carried news that the Governor would be spending opening day of Walleye season at a lake about 25 miles away. "So the governor's been up here," I asked the store clerk, pointing to the story that had been clipped and pasted on the window.

"No, that's next year."

As in 11 months, three weeks, and six days from now the governor would go fishing in their lake. That was the biggest story. For the next two days I would see other local papers giving the same front page story getting the same hallowed treatment. Complete with big color photos of the governor holding a big fish by its gills.

O.K.

Walleye season is big and lots of boats forming a Walleye armada were on the river where Bob was pointing.

Canada? He was talking about me going back to Canada? Was he insane? Didn't he know about the mystical pit bulls guarding that magical land? Ready to rip to shreds any intruder before consigning them to the gates of their fiery yet cold hell? All under the control of a woman I knew only as a number but now as Judy?

"Yeah but why would anyone want to go there," I asked. Old habits and all that.

"Easier to get a ride over there, for one," he said. "There's nobody on this road. Lots more east-west traffic on the same road just on the other side of the river."

Canada. I felt my sphincter tighten.

She would know. No law breaker was safe from her steely penetrating, walleye, waterboarding-like gaze.

"Do what you like but I'm turning off in a bit."

And I was getting out. It was empty out there. And that river was close and narrow. I could almost walk across just by going from boat to boat. I had no wish to provoke the mighty and long reach of Canadian law enforcement, but the prospect of crossing that river started looking better and better and better and ...

Steyn could not have been that wrong, could he?

HITCHIN' ON THE WALLEYE HIGHWAY.

A few minutes later I went down to the river. "Hey fellas," I said to a couple of 20-somethings on a boat close enough to the shore that I did not have to raise my voice.

"How about a lift? I'm hitchhiking around the country and writing a book on it."

If there is one thing I have learned – or maybe just remembered – on this little trip is that teens and 20-something guys will do just about anything if it promises even a hint of relief from boredom, let alone adventure.

So I got on for my three minute ride to Canada. Long enough to tell them this was my first (hitching) ride on a boat. I had started the day hoping I would hitch a ride on a plane at an air show, but I was long gone before air show organizers called me back to say they could make that happen "no problem."

On the shores of Gitchy-goomee, I also told them about Judy. The blonde, etc. And how she kicked me out. Had I the time I would have filled them in on Steyn and Steamboat Springs as well, but ....

"Yeah. She's a bitch. She lives around here, ya know. I see her all the time."

Great. They knew her too. This small town thing had its downs as well as ups. My obsession with Judy was tearing my rules to shreds. Somehow, I got away with it.

They set me down on near some rocks. Armed with directions, some slightly muddy shoes and damp back from the rain turning on and off, I set out for the Highway 11 on the Canadian side of the border.

Like most Canadian immigrants without a thoroughly documented history of Anti-Americanism and pro-Talibanism, I felt naked.

Not having time to change into my angry Muslim cleric robes to ensure a safe and easy journey to the Canadian side of International Falls, I set out with my thumb out.

In a few minutes I was on my way, and soon I was saying goodbye to one of the locals in front of a local diner. I had already given my "hitchhiking and book" story about ten times in the last few hours so I just let it go. I wanted a Canadian hamburger.

That was when I saw Judy. I'm pretty sure it was her. Out of uniform in a car. I was sitting in a booth watching fronting the street when Judy drove by. I swear she looked right at me. But she betrayed no recognition. She picked up a phone.

My international crime radar sense was tingling on high. You don't get to be an international criminal on the loose as long as I had been without a finely honed tingly radar. Just ask Carlos the Jackal.

I got up, slapped a Canadian bill on the counter that had a 20 on it, picked up my pack and headed the heck out of there. Back to the river. Which I hoped was nearby. It was.

Within 30 minutes I was back at the shore, flagging another ride. Feeling a bit more harried, I had to calm myself before asking one of the several boats for a lift back to the homeland.

I did not offer my usual story. Just thanked the guys for the lift. I faced Canada as we headed for freedom.

This was not the first time I had trouble with international borders. In 1970, in the company of other second year German students from Salesianum School, we spent three days in East

Germany. On our way, I took lots of pictures at the border. 100 miles later, soldiers came into train compartment and wanted to know who took the pictures.

I fessed up and had to hand over the film after about 30 minutes of questioning in the presence of a large German Shepherd.

In Mexico, federal police kept a companion and I in a holding cell for about three hours before we figured out they just wanted us to give them $5 "por refrescos." We did. And after trading sunglasses with the Capitan, took off on my motorcycle on the way to the Yucatan.

So I knew the drill. Judy did not look like the 'refresco' type. And Judy had no need for snarling German shepherds.

I thought it unlikely that Judy saw me, but I wanted to keep an eye out just in case. Empty or no, I was hitting the American road and saying goodbye to Canada for the second time that day.

I did not see any Walleye's. Nor did I look.

I thanked the guys and hopped out, careful not to slip in the fresh mud that was really more like overly damp dirt.

A few minutes later I was on the road, kicking the mud from my boots. I turned to wave goodbye to my liberators. They were otherwise occupied on the river.

Heading for Judy. Who was waving her arms and, and pointing at something on the other side. Which I think was me. I did not know the next time I ran into arm waving and law enforcement, at least there would be police helicopters. Looking for me.

Within ten minutes, it was raining pretty hard. I was on my way in a late model Chevy pickup into International Falls.

And away from Judy.

RADIO ON THE ROAD.

So far, the rides have been short, but easy to get. Or at least they seem short when you are enjoying the company. And easy when you have something to occupy you on the road, such as a radio where I listen and enjoy Rush, Sean, Mark Levine, even Savage and NPR.

Chapter 16

Two Carnies in Warroad, Minnesota

The Carnie test.

I can spot a carney from two counties away. And my carney senses were tingling on high when I squeezed into the tiny Suzuki that looked like some kind of toy boat.

Bill had the carney teeth and the tattoos. Though ever since crack and body art exploded on the middle class, carney spotting is a much tougher sport.

"Nice car."

"It's my mom's" said the 40 something guy. And a few minutes later: "I'm on probation for burglary."

Bingo. That clinched it: A carney.

"So what carnival did you work for?" I asked.

He looked at me for a second as if I were the barker at a Midway con game. Then he reached into his wallet and pulled out a photo of buxom, heavily made up young lady that would probably not get carded in most bars.

This was a test. A carney test.

"How old do you think she is" he asked as he studied me in the afternoon light near Warroad, Minnesota.

"13," I said without hesitation.

"Jeez, I guess you really were in the carnival."

Yeah, guess I was, back in 1974.

My stint as a carnie began over a kitchen table and a porno movie. My friends I had just flipped a coin to see if we would watch Deep Throat or Blazing Saddles. Deep Throat won. So we were off.

Thirty two-years later, I would meet the star of Blazing Saddles, Gene Wilder, on the golf course and talk with him about his newest two books. It never occurred to me to mention to him that my inability to distinguish between Deep Throat and Blazing Saddles put me on the path that brought me to him.

Two hours after the coin toss, we were walking away from the movie theater. We were not old enough to see Deep Throat so we went next door to the James E. Strates Show carnival instead.

One Help Wanted sign later and that weekend, we were gone. On the road with the carnival.

For the next five months at $65 a week, we learned about 13 year old girls who chase carnies like catnip; the world's smallest perfectly formed colored midget; the best rides for making money; the best rides for finding money; the opening lines of the first after-work conversation every new carney has with his new buddies: "So, what are you wanted for

A few hours before someone asked me and my buddy Andrew that question, one of the carnies had died when a train car dropped on him. The answer to the question: Murder in two states.

I worked the Roundup. My buddy Andy, who just a few years before had been one of Joe Biden's first clients out of law school, worked the Rock-o-Plane.

We worked 14/16 hours a day and slept under my ride. We travelled up and down the East Coast. At the end of the season, he gave us a party, where in front of his pretty daughter and 100 hungry carnies, he told us about how he would spend the off-season on his yacht.

No one heard that part. They were just looking at his daughter.

And that was that.

But Jimmy my new carney buddy and I talked more about burglary than carney life.

He caught early, he said. "Lucky," I said. "If you take the warning. Lots of burglars get addicted to burglary. They like the rush of the violation way more than the few bucks they get for your old stuff. If you look at a police report, there's a box you check if the burglar defecated in your house. That's how often they do it. Only time I ever saw that on TV was the Sopranos."

I don't think my new buddy had it that bad, not yet.

We pulled into Warroad.

"Mind if I take your picture?"

"No, not at all."

"Thanks."

Chapter 17

Apologies from International Falls

Canada keeps messin' with me.

Another first: A guy stops his car to apologize for not giving me a lift.

And then it got really strange.

"I'm sorry I can't give you a ride but I'm only going a few blocks," said the 20-something guy.

Then, with me on the side of the road and him sitting at the wheel of his on the busiest road leaving International Falls, Minnesota, we just started talking.

"I've been thinking about making some changes in my life," he said. "I just got back from Colorado."

Colin does Dr. Phil, with a side of the Dad of the Year, on the roadside, near the church, across from the bait shop, in Minnesota.

"Really? Where."

"I worked at Winter Park." Just a few miles from Loveland Ski Area.

"No kidding. I just got back from Loveland. I taught snowboarding there for a while. Everybody at Loveland really liked Winter Park. In fact, my buddy Matt Graziano taught down there. Did you know him?"

"Matt? Matt? Matt! Oh yeah."

"Liked the Grateful Dead," I suggested.

"Oh yeah, I knew Matt."

And so did he and so we talked for another five minutes before I sent him on his way. I think he said he was sorry again. I gave him a card and took his picture. I'm getting good rides from really unusual people. Not all. But most.

After Winter Park Guy took off, two brothers picked me up on their way to the local lake to fish for ...you guessed it, Walleye. I asked them about the river between Canada and the U.S. and told them a bit about my adventure South of the Border. Both of them.

INTERNATIONAL FALLS TO DULUTH.

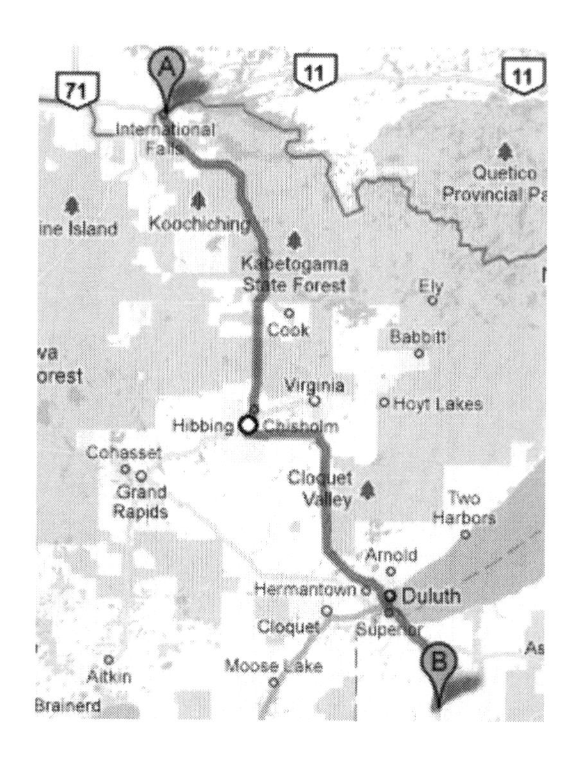

"We don't like fishing that river because it's too dirty," said the 20-year old driver. "Yeah, but anyone can walk across it, easy," said his 25-year old brother sitting in between us in the front seat of the small, Japanese pickup truck.

I took some pictures of the Brothers Fish in front of a big – you guessed it -- Walleye and before taking off, they offered me a can of Ice Tea.

"No Thanks, but I hope I see you again." And they were down the road.

The Plan.

So I have a plan: Go North, the hug the border as much as I can on the way East. Staying on the smaller roads, cross Minnesota, Wisconsin, Michigan, head to Detroit to see my buddy Todd for a day or so, then cross over the Pennsylvania to visit relatives and re-enact any family dramas that need re-enacting.

After the Brothers Fish let me out, I head into the Walleye Shrine masquerading as a country convenience store. Then amid the trees and boats of Northern Minnesota – and by the way there are more boats on the road than in the water up there – the radio goes on and the thumb goes out.

It's Saturday afternoon, and Garrison Keillor is on the radio. Alright, alright, I called him lame. But of course he's not. Of course he's funny and entertaining and relaxed and charming and that is why he is so popular even with people who do not worship earth shoes. Like me.

So this day, Keillor and his gang is presenting a radio drama about growing up and fishing and doing something funny with a fish head while everyone was supposed to be in school.

It was funny, but not that funny. Kind of off.

Then a guitar player and songwriter came out and talked about how happy he was to be on the show because "now my parents know I have a real job." And everyone laughed a bit too loud.

What the hell was going on with Prairie Home Companion?

It took me 20 minutes to find out: It wasn't the Prairie Home Companion after all but a Canadian knockoff called the Vinyl Café.

That's how they roll in Judy-land. I guess so if they are stopping all the artists at the border.

I head for Duluth through Walleye and Eagle and Doctor country.

Chapter 18

Eagle Town

Great women, remembered.

About an hour later I was spilling into a late model SUV. driven by a guy who looked about my age and height, i.e. he was older and cramped.

Turns out he was an M.D. visiting an old friend who did not have long to live. He drove from Duluth, about 100 miles to the South. Now that is what I call a house call. We were still far enough North to enjoy the trees and water and natural beauty of the Land of Ten Thousand Lakes.

"Did you see those eagles?" he said.

"Eagles? You have eagles up here. I didn't see them."

So he turned the car around and a minute later we were about 25 yards from a few dozen eagles and a whole murder of crows sitting on the railroad tracks, eating something they obviously found very, very tasty.

And oh yeah, don't forget the turkey buzzard.

Several other eagles watched from nearby trees. We watched stayed for a moment before heading down the road to Orr, Minnesota. We talked medicine and kids and Minnesota and California and hitchhiking.

Where we parted with pictures. Great guy.

Rethinking the Whole Ride Thing.

By the time I got to Orr, Minnesota, I was starting to rethink the entire trip through the small road thing. In some places, most places, it is probably easier to get rides because the cars are going slower, the drivers can see you better, and lots of people know if they do not pick you up, nobody else will.

So I thought the side roads would be slower and make it harder to get a lifts. Not so.

In Orr, Minnesota, I took lots of pictures and thought of my old friend Jack Orr who died about a year ago. I think about our mutual friend Jerome from San Diego, who sends me encouraging messages about my trip, reminding me where my home is, and what it is I do there to entertain my friends and generally justifying my existence upon this mortal coil.

I don't know why anyone would call a planet earth when you could be calling it a mortal coil.

Jerome knows a long, fragile tether when he sees one fraying.

The next few rides were uneventful, and we talked about the usual: Good friends, bad wives, and fishing, fishing, fishing. And dogs.

Outside of Orr, I sat on a dam and talked Walleye.

"Catch any Walleye?"

"Not yet."

Silence.

More silence.

"Good luck," and I was back on the road next to the river.

EX-HUSBAND OF THE YEAR ON GOOD WIVES.

When Jimmy pulled over, he also got out to check his boat. "Got into an accident last night," he said. "Coming around the corner too fast, it just fell over. I'm not going to tell my wife about it, she'll just rag me all the way home."

We stopped at an antique store to check on one of his carpet cleaning clients. “Damn, I stayed at the casino last night and lost $300.”

Dang. Tell me about it. We were back in his truck and talking dogs.

"I think I got my son in trouble once when he said they were talking in school about whether dogs have souls and whether they can go to heaven," I said. "I just repeated the old line: if there are no dogs, it is not heaven."

Hunter, the big chocolate lab, did not budge. Outside, the trees and back roads of Minnesota twisted and lifted.

Jimmy knew he was no picnic. And truth be told he wasn’t. And that was why he and his wife had almost separated several times. “But she keeps telling me she loves me, so I guess that is why I stay.”

But he did not want his wife telling him he was an idiot for crashing the boat. But that was impossible: He knew she was going to nag him about it, he was just did not want to be in a place where he could not escape from once it started.

Mr. Ex-husband of the Year weighed in. "Did you ever hear of a book called the Christmas Box?"

He shrugged. I have to stop asking people if they have read all these books as if they were spending ten hours a week at Barnes and Noble like you know who.

"It's one of the publishing phenoms today with millions of copies and movies and accessories and all that jazz. But when he wrote it, no one wanted to publish it so he did it himself, at great expense to his family's middle class budget. The way I heard him tell the story on the radio, it was sometime in the Christmas season and he came home one night after another season of unsuccessfully promoting his book. 'We're broke,' he told his wife. 'I spent everything on this book. And it's all gone.' She looked at him and said 'that's OK, think about how many lives you touched.'

Now that is a great woman. In the spirit of you can never hear enough of these stories, I told him another.

THE LEGEND OF BILLY WALTERS.

"This about the world largest sports bettor. Through one set of circumstances or another, I found myself having dinner with him in Vegas, and knew him as a successful business man, not a gambler. After dinner, he handed me a book – 'Here Colin, you like to read, check this out.' And it was a book about the world's greatest gamblers. Chapter One, my buddy Billy Walters.'

OK, so I stretched it and said he was my buddy. He knows my name, and what's a little stretching between acquaintances? Back to the great chick stories I was telling Jim the Fisherman.

"So the book talks about his life as a gambler, his ups and downs, and how won and lost and won several fortunes. The first time he ever lost it all – and not the only time – he had to wake up his wife to tell her he had just lost a million dollars and they were broke. 'That's OK, she said. 'You'll win it back.' "

"Now those are two women to swim the shark-infested seas for, to paraphrase Rabbi Laura Schlesinger."

I looked at him and he nodded, both of us wistful.

That story impressed me even more than watching Billy and his pro partner win the Pebble Beach Pro-Am on national TV. Billy could not miss any putts. Drive for show, putt for dough.

Someone smart enough to find a woman like that is someone way too smart for me to ever gamble with.

Back in the truck, Boat Crasher and I were talking dogs.

"I think I got my son in trouble once when he said they were talking in school about whether dogs have souls and whether they can go to heaven," I said. "I just repeated the old line: if there are no dogs, it is not heaven."

I did not know then that he would see St. Guinefort there as well.

Hunter, the big chocolate lab, did not budge. Outside, the trees and back roads of Minnesota twisted and lifted.

Jimmy dropped me off in front of Duluth's most famous ice cream shop, "if you like that sort of thing."

"What kind of fool doesn't like ice cream," I asked.

This is the fourth time I've been directed to a town's favorite ice cream parlor with assurances that it was the best in the country.

After taking in a very nice vanilla shake in a very cozy ice cream shop, I proceeded to walk through Cloquet, backward.

I had looked at the map and could not figure out how I was supposed to pass through Duluth and enter Wisconsin on Highway 2. There were just too many ins and outs and it seemed real confusing. I wasn't sure I'd get there before nightfall even though it was just about 20 miles away and I still had several hours of daylight.

Then I saw something I had not seen in about three weeks. A Walmart.

I even called my buddy Dan, whom I now call Base Camp, to see if he could figure out how to get to the other side of Duluth. He couldn't. It was one of those 'you can't get there from here' deals.

So I knew I would just have to stick out my thumb and hope someone who knew where they were going would pick me up and deliver me over there.

The plan was to cross Northern Wisconsin and enter the Upper Peninsula of Michigan then head down to Detroit. To do that I had to hit Highway 2, which seemed very unlikely.

MEDICINE MAN RESCUE

So after walking backwards through Cloquet, I stuck out my thumb and soon the medicine man of a local Indian tribe pulled his small pickup into the gravel. His brother jumped into a cramped back set and I poured myself into the front.

For the first time I felt a bit uncomfortable because the brother – Toad – was sitting very close behind me. But I could not see him. They were very friendly, but very close.

But soon we were jabbering. He told me he goes to other tribes in the area and conducts religious services for the Native American Church – which to me means lots of peyote. Though I did not ask. I was after all, a guest.

He had just returned from a sweat lodge in Pine Ridge South Dakota, where he conducted a coming of age ceremony for a young man.

This was the same sweat lodge that Tony Curtis advised me to visit way back in South Dakota right before I turned off for Deadwood.

"When you get there, look up the Jesuit priest who lives on the reservation," he said. "He'll fix you up."

We talked Indian stuff and after a while I had to pull out my Indian street cred. (Let me check my calendar: Yeah, that's right: It's been at last five years since people in the ghetto started using the term 'street cred' so by my reckoning it is safe for me to use it as well.')

Anyway, I told him this story.

MONIQUE, THE INDIAN CHIEF FROM HELL

This time about a year ago I got a call from Monique, the friend of an old girl friend of mine. A girl whom I still fancied a great deal. Monique was a member of a San Diego Indian tribe. That much I remembered. She had just run for tribal chair and won. But the tribal leaders said she had cheated so they declared the election null and void and decided to have another in about six weeks.

This was all a done deal by the time I got the call so fighting the election results was not an option. They are pretty much setting their own rules out there, in elections and other matters. But she wanted me to help her in the upcoming election.

So we met for lunch, and as I had asked, she brought me the paperwork which backed up everything she said. Because I knew Monique to be an untrustworthy, drug using, neglectful mother. So I needed to see it in Black and white.

She got the most votes. They said No Way.

I didn't have to ask if she had any money. I knew she did not. But I was eager to figure out a way to get closer to my old girl I'll call Scripps Ranch. If you are asking why my old girl friend was buddies with a drug addict, I cannot give you an answer other than stupidity is alive and well with all concerned.

Plus, I figured having an Indian tribe for a client could turn out to be a good gig. So there was a reason, if not a very good one.

So we got started.

Now according to Monique, the old guard was were violent, corrupt and probably even had bad table manners. There were lots of guns and drugs and all sorts of bad things on the reservation. But they did have one thing: A casino. They also had a wind farm.

So they stakes, if not high, were at least enough to get a lot of attention.

Monique's family and friends felt threatened and intimidated, so door to door was not going to work.

She was telling the truth about that.

Mail would, I told her. And did, especially among people who lived away from the reservation -- such as in some far away state prison, where some crazy percentage of the voters lived.

It was a tough election and Monique did not do a thing she said she was going to do.

So she won in a close election even after her other two opponents combined their campaign to stop her.

Now she's the boss. And her very first vote was to exempt members of the tribal council from new rules that compelled all casino employees to take drug tests.

If multiple reports of Monique raging under the influence of some kind of intoxicant on multiple occasions in the middle of the night in the middle of the reservation are true -- and they are -- she's worst than the people she replaced.

And had good reason to make that her first vote. But I did get a chance to see good ole Scripps Ranch again.

So the accounts are all cleared.

And that is what I told my new found Indian friends. They liked it enough to go way out of their way to take me to the exact spot I needed to find to make my way to where I write these words.

The Pirsig thing isn't perfect. When someone gives you a ride that takes you to a freeway it just does not make that much sense to ask to get out of the car. You just make do the best you can.

And that is what I was doing in the woods of Northern Wisconsin when my Native American buddies dropped me off at the rest stop on the big old highway.

I was checking around for sleeping and shelter arrangements while the shadows darkened and my thumb tired. Yes, thumbs get tired after sticking them out for an hour or so.

A railroad engineer stopped, and off we went into the Wisconsin night. Something about the night that brings out the bad chick stories.

"I used to be married, but I caught my wife cheating on me. I had a detective follow her and he took some pictures. A few days later we were at a wedding, her relatives. We were sitting with the guy who was screwing my wife -- and his wife. My wife got up to go the restroom when I told him I knew what was going on. And punched him in the face before beating the living shit out of him. As you can imagine, it created quite an uproar. By the time my wife came back, I took out the pictures and threw them at her. Right in front of all her relatives. That cost me three days in jail but she bailed me out."

Dang.

Now he was an engineer. Which took me a minute to figure out that he drove railroad trains. I asked him about foamers. "Oh yeah, they like trains so much and get so excited they start foaming at the mouth whenever they talk to anyone who works for a railroad. You're not supposed to, but I give them rides if I see them out there taking pictures. That is a highlight of their life."

Finally I could ask someone how to hop a train: "Don't. If they catch you, the FBI will put you in jail."

I didn't press. Mostly because this is not the kind of trip where I'm pressing for rides. Not yet anyway.

Railroad Man soon dropped me off in front of a hotel two miles off the freeway on a nice lake right in the middle of a big Wisconsin forest. The Lake in the Woods that way back, the cop told me I should visit. Soon I was watching the end of an NBA game while looking out at the moonlit lake outside my hotel window.

Still meeting lots of nice helpful people who just want to make sure I get where I am going. I'm glad Base Camp reminded me to take their pictures.

To catch up on my notes and blog entries, I stay another night. At least that is my excuse.

Another hitchhiking lesson: Whenever I can, I like to give people a nice long look at me when they are stopped or going slow -- with a nice long and inviting place to pull over. That is not what you will find most of the time.

Of course if someone told me that giving people a long look at you leads to fewer rides, I'd probably believe that too.

Chapter 19

Colin Gets Hair Cut, and other tales of snowboarding from the mountain.

The second time I copied Bruce was a hell of a lot less painful than the first.

We were both teaching snowboarding at a big resort in Colorado when Bruce showed up and announced he had just cut his own hair. He pulled off his hat to show us his newly self-shorn scalp.

We were standing outside in a blizzard. We got one just about every day, so we hardly even noticed anymore.

I was impressed.

About a week later, I was trimming my beard and said: "F' it. If Bruce can do it...I'm going to cut my own hair too."

So I set the beard trimmer to 4, and started running it all over my scalp. 15 minutes later, boom. I was clean shaven. Top and bottom.

Greetings from Loveland Resort

Three days later I discovered some kind of Alfalfa-like lick of hair sticking up on the back of my head. But other than that, no problem.

Did it again a week ago on the road. No problem. Unless you consider dragging five electronic devices each with its own charger in a small pack a problem.

No problem. The first time I tried to copy Bruce – now that was a problem. A painful problem.

I had moved to Colorado to do some snowboarding and ended up almost by accident teaching the sport at Loveland resort, 11,000 feet up on top of the continental divide.

When I applied, I did not pretend to be the world's greatest snowboarder. And that is what I told them. But I did say I was a decent teacher so there I was, one of ten new instructors getting ready for his three days of on-the- mountain training.

I had learned to snowboard 13 years before, and it was tough. Brutally tough. I would have walked off many times but I did not want my kids to see me quit. I thought I had to show them their old man still had a trick or two up his sleeve.

I fell down a lot but after two years and lots of bruises, one day I found myself cruising down a slope listening to Bruce Springsteen's Thunder Road on the loudspeakers, suddenly realizing: "hey, I can do this."

Now that I think about it, the slope was kind of flat. But my self regard was flat out 90 degrees straight up.

I could snowboard! And over the next six years that is what I convinced myself with and without my kids on slopes all over California and Utah.

At Mammoth Mountain, I took a wrong turn to an intermediate slope and ended up staring over the edge of cliff called the Corniche Bowl. Black Diamond. Double, I think. It seemed like a triple.

If I could have, I would have walked off. But that was not an option. Going back was not physically possible.

To get on the slope, you actually had to climb under an overhanging cliff. Thus the bowl.

As I peeked over the edge, all I could see was a sheer cliff side as close to 90 degrees as you can get. Halfway down the slope, several pairs of skis stuck out like cemetery markers. About ten stories below, I heard some tiny skier shouting: "Hey dude, can you get my skis?"

"Noooo."

Finally I got on what can loosely be called the slope and the mountain was just about a foot from my face. And I began slipping, sliding, clawing and falling down the mountain. With maybe a turn or two. The snow was soft so falling was no big deal.

Eventually I reached the bottom: It had been some kind of religious experience. Strong enough that I convinced myself that I was a competent, if not good, snowboarder.

My snowboarding suffered after my kids got out of high school and I started playing golf twice a week. So by the time I reached Loveland for my interview, I had only been on my board about once a year for the last 6 years.

But after getting hired for "my enthusiasm," I had about a month to get my board legs back. No problem, I thoughtAs much as I tried, it did not happen. I was a lousy snowboarder. And we were getting ready for three days snowboarding down slopes that – after Corniche Bowl – were way steeper than anything I had ever successfully navigated.

I even had trouble with the lifts. So much so that it became some kind of mental block getting off the lift. That is where you can get beat up. And I did.

So for three days, we just rode the lifts to the top of steep mountains, then talked. Then rode down about a third of the way, then talked. Then repeated till we were at the bottom then we did it again.

I did not make any excuses. It would not have done any good if I had. But after about five minutes, it was clear there were 9 people in our group who knew how to board, loved to board, lived to board.

Then there was me.

I was ready to ignore the scorns and cajoling of Bruce and the rest of the 20-somethings for whom each hill was not steep enough while I did the best I could to follow them down. I was always way behind. Falling and hurting.

But everyone pretended not to notice. A couple guys including Bruce even tried to board with me to give me a few tips (hey dude, you've got too much weight on your back foot. Which is just about the equivalent of telling a basketball coach that the object of the game is to put the ball in the hoop.)

They kind of adopted me. The teacher even told us that it was good to have me around because I was a good example of how sometimes in a class one of the students falls behind. Happy to help.

"Hey guys," I told the folks who ran the school, "I know I'm not that good, so if you don't want to keep me around, I understand."

They looked at me as if they did not know what I was talking about. "We don't need you to be a great boarder, just a good teacher." And in all the time I was there, I did not detect one rolled eyeball, one chuckle, one anything that was directed at my crappy snowboarding skills.

They did give me a ration – took the piss out of me, I think the expression is – for driving a Jag to work in the snow. That was scarier than Corniche Bowl because for a good part of the ten mile commute, I was not really driving, I was just trying to control the skids and go fast enough that I could drift through any trouble spots.

Bruce pushed me out of trouble more than once.

Between the car and the falling, I let that take a lot more of the enjoyment out of my time there than I should have.

After three days of falling I mean following Bruce down the Mountain, I began to teach.

What the hell is an Ollie?

In spite of myself, I did get a lot better. I taught mostly kids but some adults. I never really liked the part of snowboarding where you kept one foot out of the board. But after teaching for a while, that is all I did. Just moved around the school and the mountain with only one foot strapped in.

No big deal.

During the training, I sat next to a guy with a Maryland cap on. "Hey, I was born right up the road in Delaware," I told Andrew.

"Yeah, I used to room with a guy from Delaware and visit his family in the summer at Rehoboth."

"What's their name?"

"Quinn."

"Hmmm, I know some Quinns. Do you know the names of his parents?"

The next day he told me: "Kevin and Kelly."

Who are of course one of my big buddies from high school and one of my sister's best friends as well. They even visited me in California in 1977.

That was weird. Anyway, back to the slopes.

There was some hard work involved. But the novelty of being outside in the all snow and trees and altitude never wore off.

And every once in a while when I reached someone and convinced them they could be a good snowboarder, that was very gratifying.

But I was still having trouble getting off the lift.

Prior to my first lesson I knew I could not let my level 2 student see me fall. I kept thinking positive. Visualizing. All those things. And sure enough, my first lift on my first lesson I hit the ground hard.

I immediately turned over and got on my knees as if I were just getting into a better position to see my two students who were following two chairs behind. I'll be damned if both of them did not come off that lift like smooth and silky and balanced rockets.

"You guys did that better than I did," I laughed. And so did they, thinking I was kidding. I was not.

Anyway, for two hours we went up and down the mountain, and within an hour both were telling me they liked it how I did not push them and gave them lots of encouragement and that I was the best teacher they had so far.

I said thanks. And that was that.

A few days later, a nine year old boy was mildly unhappy with me because I would not teach him "an Ollie."

"What they hell's an Ollie?" I wondered to myself.

"No Ollie till the second lesson. We're going to work on basics."

"I bet you don't even know how to do an Ollie," he said.

"Of course I do. But not today. Big Dog."

"You call everybody Big Dog."

It went like that sometimes.

After the season, Bruce and his girlfriend headed off to Hawaii. He's a boat captain and wants to get back into that.

I told him I was a marketing guru and could get his boat more attention in more places than he would believe.

I'd dangle a thousand bleeding fish in front of a thousand starving sharks before I confront one more Black Diamond.

Chapter 20

Dylan in the Rearview Mirror

Mission change. Sorry Solon.

Today was going to be different. Today there would be no lollygagging. No meandering from town to town; ride to ride; hotel TV to hotel TV.

Today I had a mission: I had 8 days to get to San Francisco – 2200 miles away. A client called and wanted to talk to me about giving me lots of money for small amounts of indoor work with no heavy lifting.

I may have neglected to mention to him that his high-priced media guru, the guy who got him in the New YorkTimes, the Wall Street Journal, and hundreds of other media outlets both print and electronic, local and national; the guy whom he fired once for telling his other executives they didn't know anything about anything; was hitchhiking around the country.

So I had to get a move on.

My new found focus would be tested right away.

I left Solon Springs, Wisconsin bright and cold and early. 11 a.m. But not before noticing Northern Wisconsin is just about the most beautiful part of the whole darn country.

By noon I was climbing into my first car. Jim was a process server and M-1 tank driver.

"You get one of those M-1's doing 55 miles per hour in the woods and nothing can stop you… there's nothing like it."

I wondered if we could drive one to California. So I asked him where he lived.

"Hibbing."

He did not have to say Minnesota. Ever since I was a teenager I have always associated Minnesota not with the Vikings or some lame politico, but with Hibbing. The birthplace of Bob Dylan. And I never really even considered myself that big of a fan.

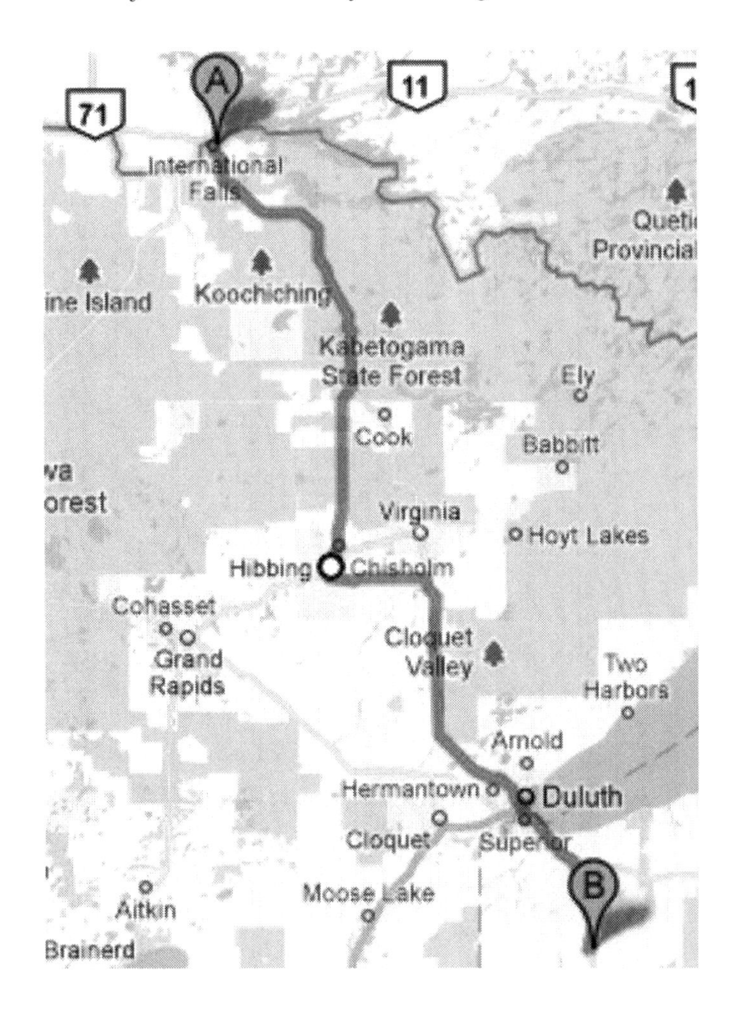

Yesterday, every local paper in the region was running big stories about Bob Dylan days, five days away.

Damn. Damn. Damn. I said to Jim:

"I passed Hibbing yesterday and I really wanted to stop for a few days. And that was before I found out about the big party this weekend. I'm not a fanatic but I am a fan. But I can't. I have to be on my way."

The situation was about to go from bad to worse.

The M-1 tanker drew a bead on me. "You sure you can't go? I'm going right back there after I serve these papers. You can stay at my house."

Damn. Damn. Damn.

I was eager to go to San Francisco on business. But ... well, you can be eager and happy about two things at once, can't you?

"Can't. Want to. Can't. "I tried without success to change the subject. "People in Hibbing like Dylan?"

"Yeah but not that much. I live a block from where he was born. I've lived there for a few years and took me a while to figure out why so many people were outside taking pictures all the time."

The guy is the greatest poet of the 20th century. If Crazy Horse can get himself a statue with an 80-foot face, Dylan deserves something. At least a visit.

Damn.

After 15 miles the Master of War pulled over. "Last chance."

"No. Damn it."

Now meandering across America 15 miles at a time is fine if you have nowhere to go. But at this rate I'll be three weeks late for San Francisco.

"I'll be back this way in 30 minutes. Maybe you'll change your mind."

For the next 29 minutes I thought about Hibbing and Desolation Row and Highway 61 and Tangled Up in Blue and Blood on the Tracks and Dylan going electric and how Steven Stills said the greatest poet of the 20th century "was not a musician."

And how someone like Dylan could spring up fully blown from the prairies and woods of Hibbing. I'm sure lots of Dylan fans would say 'how could he spring up from anywhere else?'

Dylan going electric and having all these folkie hippies try and jeer him from the stage is one of the great musical moments of our age.

With my Titleist golf cap gleaming white in the 45 degree morning sun, my dreams of Hibbing disappeared when a golf course manager on his way to work pulled over.

My First Mayor -- of Superior.

"I was the mayor of Superior," he said. I'm pretty sure that was up the road a stretch in Minnesota.

"D or R," I wanted to know.

"D," he smiled knowingly. "You must be too," he said, knowing for sure that only a Democrat would be goofy enough to go hitchhiking around the country. "Being from San Diego and all."

I dodged that question by asking him how he liked being mayor. "I liked it, but no one ever thanks you. That's for sure. They're always waking you up at 2 in the morning to fix parking tickets."

I nodded. As if I knew what he was talking about. Come to think of it, I kind of did, having worked for lots of people holding public office.

It was time to play my Big Dog Democratic Card on him, that with any luck would impress him so much he would just keep driving his late model GM luxury car all the way to California with his new best friend perched in the front seat.

I've been playing this card since 1972 and no one ever cared. I knew my luck was bound to change and this time would be different.

So now you do not have to wonder why casinos keep sending me free hotel rooms.

"I've worked for a lot of politicians. Speech writing. Column writing. Opposition research." The last two words I said slowly and carefully while making air quotes in front of me.

Using the term opposition research is the linguistic equivalent of standing over a bullet ridden corpse and pronouncing the cause of death as "lead poisoning."

But I was just warming up.

"One of the more interesting campaigns I ever worked on was in 1972 when I met a young guy running for U.S. Senate against one of the most popular politicians in our state. He was a lawyer for the local juvenile delinquents. I knocked on some doors with him and brought him to my church on Sunday's for a coffee and donut fundraiser between masses. Say, whatever happened to that guy Joe Biden anyway?"

Bam!

He didn't flinch. He saw my Biden and raised me a Mondale and a Humphrey. Both of whom he knew very well.

I tossed my card face down and flicked them towards the dealer.

I told him I had just read about his buddy Mondale's daughter being very sick. I wanted to ask him what she was really doing during all those private visits with Clinton in the White House. Bill Clinton, that is.

With Democrats you never know.

But I didn't ask. The Opposition Researcher was coming out. Old habits and all that.

We moved to safer ground. He had been to Augusta National to see the greatest golf tournament in the world. I had been to St. Andrews, to play the greatest course in the world.

I had been playing golf twice a week – and practicing at least that much -- for the last 15 years before I left for Colorado in December.

I did not miss it as long as I was walking on 96 inches of powder-topped snow.

But seeing the empty and glowing green rolling hills of a newly green golf course made my fingers twitch.

To yearn. That is what it means.

By now I was beginning to take the beautiful hills and trees and country-side of Northern Wisconsin for granted. Which is a mistake because that's some fine space up there.

I imagined my golf clubs in my son's garage. The one who thinks I'm an asshole. I had no idea how I was going to get them. Couldn't worry about that now. I checked my watch after saying goodbye to the mayor and promising to stay in touch.

Chapter 21

The Ballad of St. Guinefort

Colin Gets and Gives a Free Lunch

I said goodbye to the mayor and hello to the Preacherman. He moved his fishing rods out of the way.

We talked about books and family and kids and Wisconsin. And how I thought Northern Wisconsin was the prettiest part of the country I had ever seen. Lots of lakes.

"Way nicer than Colorado," I said.

"Come on I'll buy you lunch in my hometown."

Sounded good. It's time I started making this hobo thing start working for me. I didn't realize by the end of the day it would get out of hand.

We talked about marketing and how marketers for the new mega churches were usually way better than the ones I had met in the corporate world. He had a new church with 130 members and was curious about how tactics and strategy from my world could be used in his.

So I gave him my spiel.

Every new organization or idea or cause has to show to things: 1) It is good. 2) It is popular.

Most people concentrate on the first and ignore the second. That is one good reason why most new things fail.

So here's the challenge: Imagine the ideal. Then create it.

To do this, you have to ask this question: If your church were popular, really popular, what would that look like?"

"Would there be stories and pictures of your church members in local papers?"

"Would they write letters to the editor?"

“Would the pastor write columns and appear on talk radio applying theology to issues of the day, big and small?"

"Would church members call talk radio?"

"Appear on Cable TV?"

"Yes. Yes. Yes. Yes. and yes. Imagine the ideal. Then create it. Am I gabbing too much?"

"No. No. this is fascinating."

Yes, he actually said that. I had his full attention.

"Alright, I'll gab for a bit more: It's all about the school yard. Let's say the popular kids are on one side. The smart kids the other. We look at the popular kids and think 'those kids are good.' Now look at the smart kids. Does anyone think they are popular? Or even good? No."

We jabbered on through tomato bisque and half a sandwich. Even out in the places where you can't find a Walmart or a Starbucks, you can find a decent bowl of soup.

The preacher was worried that the wrong kind of marketing could alienate his church members. "Absolutely. You cannot separate methods from goals. The Medium is the message and all that. No is one is saying this should be hard sell.”

I continued: But how about this: Get a list of every person who moves to within 10 miles of your church."

"You can do that?" he asked.

"Oh yeah, that's marketing 101. Have some kids knock on their door with a welcome basket and invitation to a service or a party for new members. You gotta ask for the sale. Every good salesman knows that. He may not know anything else, but he knows that. Hard sell or soft sell, that's how it works."

Preacherman was a young guy. About 30. But he got it.

Preacherman had planned to rope, tie and brand me as a Jesus loving man after he picked me up. But after I mentioned in an off hand way that someone else had tried that for 200 miles just a few days before, he backed off.

And I'm glad he did because I got to learn about him and his family and how he was a wrestling coach and how I should stay with his family if I ever return to Northern Wisconsin.

He told me about the only Fortune 500 company in the area, and how they used to make hamburger patties for McDonald's, till that went away and it almost went out of business.

It stayed alive with beef jerky.

"Businessmen don't get enough credit for being people of faith," I suggested. "That company had no guarantees their jerky would sell. But they went for it in an act of faith that would humble some of the apostles. Great businessmen are often men of great faith," I suggested, preaching to the preacher.

"And that is really your challenge as a preacher to show how great faith can be an important part of our every day lives -- a way to improve them. You remember that scene from the bible when God sends Mannah to the Jews in the desert with only one caveat: Just take enough for today."

"This is also a reason why some Christians believe insurance is a form of gambling and should be shunned."

Ned Flanders.

Ok, so I was jabbering in overdrive. But this was the first cup off coffee I could not see through in weeks. So I was feeling it. Preaching to the preacherman. Soon I would be telling a crack addict what to do with chemicals. Jees.

"You seem pretty familiar with the bible for someone who is 'on the bench,' " he said.

"Twelve years of Catholic school will do that."

I thought about the Biden story and how I had dropped it to no effect just a few moments before. So I doubled down and decided to go nuclear with Preacherman. We were on our way out and he was on his way home while I would continue down the Badger state.

ST. GUINEFORT, PATRON SAINT OF UNCOLLECTED BAR BETS.

"If you have a moment I tell you my favorite religious story. Its about St. Guinefort."

Preacher man was either very interested or performing a corporal act of mercy by humoring me.

"A few years ago was at a party where people were talking about Catholic saints and rituals. I chimed in with the history of the term 'devil's advocate" and how it was applied to a person whom the Church appointed to represent the case against the person whom was being put up for sainthood.'

I can't say anyone either knew that or was impressed that I knew it. But that had started 30 minutes before when of the 15

people at the party, 14 were convinced all Republicans should be in jail for religious and economic crimes.

And then there was me. Loudmouth.

"Any of course my favorite saint was Guinefort. He was left in charge of a king's infant son while the king went off hunting. Upon returning, the king found Guineforth and his son covered in blood and killed Guinefort, thinking he had injured his son. But the blood was from a snake nearby that Guinefort killed, saving the son."

They looked at me, waiting for the other shoe to drop before they expressed their disappointment.

"And by the way, Guinefort is not only a saint, he is also the only saint who happens to be a dog. A canine."

The couch sprang to life. "That's not true," they said, rising to the bait. This was too easy. There was a computer in the next room over. And before I left to Google it for the Doubting Thomases, I thought I would do the gentlemanly thing and offer them a wager.

Just $5 on the outcome of this theological discussion.

They agreed.

Two minutes later I was back. "OK, its on the computer screen in the other room. The story of St. Guinefort. Can I have my money now?"

I knew they would be the type I would have to ask. And even then probably not get it.

And three minutes later three of them were back. Irritated with good ole Colin.

"Can I have my $5 dollars now?"

They didn't hear my first request and didn't hear the second. I'm still waiting and those folks are probably still pissed off.

But it was OK with Preacherman. And we said goodbye.

Chapter 22

Colin Loses His Phone Out on Highway 61. Forever.

It was easily done.

I missed Hibbing and did not much like that.

Not just because I would not see the old record store where Bob Dylan lost his virginity, or anything like that, but because so far I had been 'sailing with the wind," as one my benefactors had put it.

Going happily where it took me. But that part of the trip was over. At least for now. And that made it a much different trip.

A phone call had summoned back to California to ply my trade. Which was fine by me because I had somewhere around $2000 left, and it was going fast.

I was in the middle of nowhere, heading to somewhere. And the 50-something guy in a minivan was the next to send me on my way.

"Where you headed?"

California."

The further away I was from the beaten path the funnier people found this response. He was laughing. So we talked California and how I was disappointed to miss Hibbing.

For the next half hour we were just a couple of Dylan fans, appreciating the big dog. "I read his book last year," said my new pal in Dylan-dom. "I didn't like it."

"Me neither. But I knew when I bought it that it was probably going to be some ambiguous Dylan bullshit. Which works just fine in a song but not for 200 pages in a book. But no one really expected Dylan to write an autobiography that people like me would use as a travel guide through the back streets of Hibbing."

He nodded. "I'm giving my daughter the complete works of Dylan for graduation in a few days," he said.

By now, we were buds, so I had just had to know, polite or not: "Is this one of those gifts that the dad is going to like more than the daughter. You know, like Homer Simpson giving his wife a bowling ball with the initials HJS on it for their anniversary."

He laughed. Between Dylan and the Simpsons, that pretty much covers the entire range of human experience.

"No she really likes him."

I could believe that. It took my kids a while to get Dylan. Talk about protests. Jeez. They hated him, at first and whined when I played him on our way to snowboard trips. But not as much as they hated the 27-minute live version of Whipping Post. Surely I do not have to tell you that was the Allman Brothers.

My Dylan buddy pointed out the window: "Hey look, its highway 61." He paused and then looked over. "You probably want to get on that," he said, knowing that was out of my way and would cut down our time together by 150 miles.

And no he was not just trying to get rid of me.

"Yeah, I can't turn that down."

Ten minutes later, he was giving me a wistful look at he dropped me off near St. Paul under a sign that proclaimed "Highway 61."

I did not know if it was the road of song. People in Minnesota did not think it was that cool anyway. So there you have it.

There would be no Dylanesque adventures on this road. Not on this day.

I was singing Highway 61 to myself over and over when a grouchy guy pulled over and took me 175 miles into Iowa, complaining most of the way about his son who complained too much.

Come to think of it, the Father-Son conflict was Highway 61 all over. So maybe this was dylanesque after all. That guy did not care for his son, that is for sure.

Soon we stopped for a soda.

"I got it," he said, taking the bottle from my hand.

Thirty miles later he was telling me about how he hauled recreational boats around the country and how he had just made $2500 on his last trip. Then he dropped this out of nowhere: "Yeah, I bought you that soda because you look like you don't have any money."

Shit.

I did a quick self-assessment. Clean shoes. Freshly washed socks and shirts and underwear. Deodorant? check. Cologne. check. Why did he think I was a hobo?

Two days later I think I figured it out: it was the hat. It was pretty dirty. Rogaine build up.

I did not feel like getting into a discussion of my finances with this guy. Nor did I want to pull out my bankroll and show him this hobo was carrying a few ducats. I remembered visiting a trial as a requirement for some Boy Scout merit badge and some guy had gotten into knife fight because he had pulled out his bankroll and showed everyone what a big man he was.

I resolved then never to do that.

So I didn't. If this guy wanted to think I was hobo, a guy 'scrounging his next meeee-aaaaallllll,' well I decided I would let that feee-eeeelll ok.

But I did not want to be a hobo. I still had a few middle class hangups about success and self-sufficiency.

The terrain had flattened out a bit, and trees were sparser as we crossed into Iowa.

Soon enough my grouchy boat-toting friend was dropping me in the middle of a small town. I keep expecting someone to set some apple pie and milk in front of me, just as some big buy asks if I wanted to give him a hand bailing hay for a few days. "It's honest work," he would say.

Just a few months before, I was helping a kid with his snowboard and I noticed he was from Iowa. So I asked him about Field of Dreams and if he had ever heard famous line,: "Is this heaven? No it's Iowa."

Unbeknownst to me, the resort owner was standing over my shoulder. "I'm going to make you employee of the month for that," he said.

Kevin Costner keeps intruding into this narrative.

Back to reality.

My next ride was only 15 minutes, but while I was in the mini-van of this suburban housewife returning from the grocery store, I thought I was just another suburban guy getting a ride to the soccer game.

That didn't last long.

MY PHONE, GONE FOREVER. (I WANTED THE PICTURES, NOT THE PHONE.)

The next ride was two women, tattered car, a bit rough around the edges but that was just fine as far as I was concerned.

"Are you a criminal or a murderer?" Jenny wanted to know. "You don't have any weapons or anything like that do you?"

I looked at them at wondered the same thing: They wore hardcore tats and piercings like employee of the month awards.

Jenny and her sister had passed me by then come back. Lots of people do that. I wonder how many come back and I am not there.

It probably happens. I had two people stop for me at the same time up near Canada.

This was the first time Jenny's sister had ever picked up a hitchhiker. At that point, she had more nose piercings than hitchhikers.

So I tried to make it pleasant, which it was.

After they let me off, I discovered I had left my IPhone in their car. As with all my rides, I dropped off a card with my name and email on it.

Within a few hours, they were dropping a message into my MySpace page that they had my phone and would return it right away.

And in that town in Northeast Iowa was the last place I saw my Iphone. They said they would send it. Never did.

Iowa had somehow swallowed Highway 61. But my career as a hobo had at least one more ride to go.

He was a rancher. Big property owner. With a big truck and trailer he used for hauling big animals worth a lot of money. He spent a lot of time in California where he and wife owned part of a restaurant.

Any Haystacks 'Round These Parts?

He had working man hands. Even rich guys work in these parts.

"So where are you sleeping? Under a bridge?"

I laughed. But he was serious. The sun would set in about an hour and I think he was expecting to find me asleep in one of his hay stacks come dawn.

"Hotels," I told him.

He did everything he could to suppress his look of incredulity. He almost succeeded. He dropped me at the entrance to his ranch and said he would give me a lift to town when he returned in half an hour. I gave him a card just in case and suggested he could follow Colin's Big Adventure on my myspace page.

"So you really think you are going to get a ride in the next 30 minutes?"

I was after all in the middle of nowhere on a small road where there was no traffic.

"You never know."

His wave and his smile were still lingering when less than two minutes later a farm equipment repairman pulled over.

"Sometimes when we need a part we just make it, right there, on my truck. That's why I carry that welder with me," he said. I turned around and sure enough, there it was. Though he probably called it was it really was, and not welder, like some ignorant city kid like me would imagine it was called.

"I just did that for a chopper before I picked you up."

It took me at least ten minutes before I figured out he was not talking about helicopters but real farm machines that chopped things. I had no idea what farmers chopped, only that I was pretty certain there was a lot of it.

I congratulated myself on my new and keen insights into the Iowa farm life. And resolved to tell everyone about it in three years during the next Iowa caucuses.

He was only going a mile, he said, but between then and there he decided to take me another nine miles into town to the front door of my hotel.

This hobo was bunking down for the night.

Chapter 23

Iowa Gets on my Nerves for a while anyway.

I was getting ready to trash Iowa.

It was not about the hobo thing. I didn't blame that on Iowa anyway. But the minute I crossed into Iowa, signs started telling me what to do. My favorite was a big sign at my hotel that said Iowa law banned anyone from setting the automatic timer on the hot tub for more than 15 minutes.

Signs, signs, everywhere signs.

And the cop thing was getting old.

I had just left hobo central and decided my chances of getting a ride would be better if I walked past the cemetery. I have not done any scientific research on the topic of getting rides near graveyards, so call it an educated guess. Superstition, if you choose.

In Wisconsin, every ten miles is a lake. In Iowa, every ten miles I passed a graveyard. That was OK. I'm one of those people who can spend an afternoon looking at tombstones if they are old enough.

Like the ones outside of Concord, Massachusetts, which all seemingly bore the same inscription: Listen my friends, dry up your tears, for here I shall lie till Christ appears.

I had forgotten about that little hitchhiking adventure. Which is just as well because it basically would probably put the entire male faculty of a New England High School in jail for fraternizing with their pretty young students.

Ten minutes past the graveyard a big, shiny car rolled slowly to a stop in front of me. I picked up my bag, thinking what a great day it was going to be now that big, shiny cars were stopping for me first thing on such a great sunny day in the middle of nowhere Iowa.

It was a cop.

"Did you know hitchhiking was against the law?"

I looked at him, and shook my head no.

Great. First I was a hobo. Then a criminal. Then a criminal hobo. Now this cop thought I was some kind of legal scholar, particularly schooled in the rights of pedestrians on public thoroughfares.

I liked being a hobo better.

I didn't ask if he was referring to local, state, county or other laws. I figured I would be better off not knowing.

I didn't say another word. I just looked at him as if we were playing Texas hold 'em. Not the game with my buddy's Filipino family two Thanksgivings ago where I got cleaned out so quickly and thoroughly I thought I had just been through some kind of gang rape.

The game before that, I took them down. Yeah.

My short answer was my way of throwing a few chips onto the table to start the game. He would call, fold, or raise to force me out. I was bluffing and he probably knew it. He looked back. We both had weak hands because in the middle of nowhere Iowa neither of us had any more options than we did just a few minutes ago.

He called me. "Come on in. I'll give you a ride to the other side of the county.'

Turns out he was a California boy who found the good life in Iowa ten years before. A hitchhiker himself, and like the four other cops who had stopped me in the last few weeks, a very good guy who was interested in my book and wanted to help get me on my way.

An hour later, I was in another county, playing the same game with another cop, with the same result.

But soon enough a real person picked me and we headed for the Interstate. He was an insurance salesman who also owned a fitness center and tanning salon in Grand Rapids. (I think.)

Young. Married. Very bright. Another companion in whose life I saw inspiration.

Twenty miles into our 100 mile ride he wondered out loud how he could get more exposure for his salon. So for the next 30 miles I told him.

Same spiel as the Preacherman, with one added attraction. "Radio people love free stuff. If you start handing out free tans down there to the DJ's and other station folks, maybe as part of some promotion where tans are the reward for a radio contest, they will not be able to stop talking about you. Same with gym memberships."

HIS SON AND THE PARKERSBURG TORNADO

And that is true, true true.

"We're getting close to Parkersburg," he told me. "That's where the tornado set down and killed a bunch of people last year. It was all over the news." Though I did not really remember it. We were one day away from the one year anniversary of it.

"Wish I had a chance to check it out," I said. And I did. Wish that it is. But I was on my way to my own tornado in beatific Marin County California. And I could not wander. Not anymore.

Which is what I told the next guy as well when he told me about Parkersburg. "My son and 16 other people crammed into the bathroom of a Pizza Hut and the whole building collapsed around them. But not the bathroom. They were all safe."

Now he was getting ready for his senior year of football as a wide receiver and defensive back. The same team his dad played for back in the day. (As I sit to rewrite my notes from my time in

Parkersburg, the news tells us that coach of his football team was gunned down in the school weight room three weeks after I passed through.)

"If he learns how to juggle, he'll have the best hands for miles around." And I told him how when I played basketball as a kid I had terrible hands. Jimmy White, the best basketball player in my neighborhood in a generation, told me once in exasperation "you have hands like a chicken" after one of his perfect passes bounced off my fingers.

"That is not what a bounce pass is supposed to do. But after I got a book and taught myself how to juggle, I could feel my fingers surround footballs and basketballs. Almost always caught them."

Soon the Parkersburg water tower appeared in the distance, and after declining an invitation to visit, we parted as friends.

I was back in the middle of nowhere. Except this time on a huge highway with lots of cars going very long distances at a very high rate of speed. There was hope for Marin yet.

Which lasted about 15 minutes when another Iowa cop pulled up.

"Blah blah blah," I said. I was getting sick of saying it but he thought that was pretty cool as he frisked me, took my license and invited me into the front of his car. I was clean.

"I just got a report of Black Escalade weaving all over the road. But he got away. Then I got a call that you were out here and so here I am," he volunteered.

Dang. Someone called? "Hey sheriff, we got a hobo out there on highway 20. Better check him out. He's got a dirty cap too," I imagined.

Dang. Dang. Dang. So much for Midwestern self reliance and all that. These folks were control freaks. As the trip got longer, so did my sense of entitlement. Occupational hazard, I suppose.

I was kind of irritated, not at him, but just at the idea that someone would take the time to do that. I was careful not to show it. I didn't need to travel to Iowa to find out what happens when a cop thinks you are giving him a bad attitude.

"Come on, I'll give you a lift up to the next county," he said. Which was nice since that was right on my way, right on the main road. Then I saw a little but bright light appear over his head. "If you're writing a book, you've got to check out Parkersburg."

He had me. So he changed directions and off we went – down a squiggly side road.

Soon I was getting the tour from the back of a copy car of the snapped telephone poles, demolished buildings, uprooted trees and all the rest. Only most of the damage was gone.

These hard working fools had already put almost everything back together. And in the middle of the Iowa prairie, it seemed strange to see these gleaming new buildings sprouting out of nowhere.

But that is the way they roll in Iowa.

This was just about the only time I had seen brick and mortar during the entire trip. So, however temporarily, I decided to cut Iowa a break.

On the way North through Minnesota, I saw an idle train and told the cop giving me a ride that I hoped to hop on one before the summer was over. "You won't hop on that one, that's been sitting there for weeks."

And from the back of the cop car I watched for 7 miles as we drove next to the train tracks with idle and empty cars. Soon our paths split, and the train stretched into the distance as far as I could see.

Before and after Minnesota, I've seen lots of empty trains, rental yards bulging with heavy equipment, trucking company parking lots that could not take another cab, tourist attractions with no lines. And on and on.

Lots of waiting and wondering, but above all waiting.

It's like I'm playing along with the Atlas Shrugged. This world is slowing down.

Chapter 24

Colin Settles a Bet

Judge and jury: me.

Whatever else Parkersburg, Iowa, was, it was also about the 25th town I had seen walking backward with my thumb out.

Soon, for what seemed like the 25 time, some guys had to juggle fishing rods to make way for the hobo, criminal, law expert disguised as a hitchhiker.

This was different. These guys would call on my skills as a judge.

"We just got off work," said Rod. "We're going camping." I did not know what they did but Rod the driver was the ringleader. He introduced us all with handshakes all around. "Wanna beer? Sorry I can't offer you something to eat."

"That's OK. I'm good. But thanks."

Ten minutes later we were all jabbering about Iowa and fishing and Walleyes and all sorts of things. All comfortable when Rod the Driver turned around.

"I got to ask you a question: Who is more friendly. People in the Midwest. Or other people?" Thankfully he turned back to the road, if only to fish out another beer from the bag between his seats.

That was right in my wheel house.

"That's easy. People in the Midwest. No contest."

And he looked over to a guy I would later learn was his cousin from Pennsylvania, recently arrived. Rod poked him in the side. "Told ya." He looked back at me. "He just moved here."

I took that as an invitation. And it was.

If Quaker boy needed some schooling from the mysterious stranger, I was up for it. So I pressed on.

"People in the MidWest are also smarter. They know how to do more stuff, like mechanics and plumbing and carpentry and roofing."

"That's what we are, roofers. Stay Dry roofers."

"They also work harder. Even rich people work out here," I said, remembering all the big ranchers with big rusty hands who had given me rides.

"I was born on the East Coast, lived on the West, and that is what I've seen," I said to Quaker boy. I didn't talk about Southerners. That's a different kind of friendly, just as good, but different.

The driver and the guy in the back next to me could not have been happier. I think I had just settled once and for all something they had been jawing about ever since Quaker boy joined the roofing crew a few weeks back.

Quaker boy smiled and volunteered: "I work. I work sitting in front of my computer all day."

"Out here," I said, as if I were some kind of guy who also knew what it meant to work sunup to sundown then look forward to the next day when of course I was not even close to that unless working on a computer counted. "That ain't work."

They all nodded their head, drank some beer, and wondered what else they would talk about on their holiday camping and fishing trip they were taking in their work truck with their work buddies and their work provisions.

Chapter 25
Colin Finds Religion

I did after all promise to read one chapter from the Book of Proverbs every day for a month. As thanks for the ride into Fargo. After falling behind, I read about five in one sitting.

(I'm writing this in a Jack in the Box in Ukiah, north of San Francisco, where everyone now thinks I am a Jesus freak.)

The Proverbs are different than what I thought. So far I've been reading about an "adultress with seductive words…"

"From the lips of an adultress drip honey."

"The smooth tongue of the wayward wife."

"Do not lust in your heart after her beauty or let her captivate you with her eyes." (So that's where Jimmy Carter got that.)

"The adultress preys on your very life."

It goes on and on. And here I was expecting 'a penny saved is a penny earned." I found Dr. Ruth instead.

Chapter 25 -- The Sequel

The hitchhiking, rambling champ of all time takes me to Des Moines.

The next day, Pedro was pulling out as I reached over to shut his door. "Let's go, got to get to Des Moines," Which I guessed was about 100 miles away.

I looked over and discovered I was getting a ride from a full blown, tattooed and mustachioed, LA-style gang banger.

This should be interesting. But it wasn't dangerous or threatening.

"I'm from Honduras. I left there when I was nine years old, with three other guys from my neighborhood. My mom was dead and my dad was gone. So we hitchhiked from Honduras through Mexico to the border at McAllen, Texas. It took two years. About two weeks after we started the old guy of the group, my 15-year old cousin, decided he wanted to go back."

I looked over at him and at the red lipstick tattoo that jutted out from the right side of his neck towards me. He was now a 30-year old man with big hands that had done a lot of hard work, not gang banging.

"He wanted to take the money with him, but we jumped him and took it back. We walked and hitchhiked, stopping along the way to work. But within a few months, I was all by myself. But I still kept going. I was afraid my grandmother would kick my ass if I turned around."

If he had an accent, it was slight. And His story came out smooth and pure and easy.

"When I got to McAllen, I crossed the border no problem. But soon I got into trouble and they put me in a foster home. I left when I was 16."

There were gangs and drugs and trips to Los Angeles and trouble with the law. But in his early 20's he found himself in the middle of Iowa, determined to straighten himself out. Which is what he did when he learned how to drive a truck.

Now he is a citizen. He and his buddies are always doing something: Sculpting, or really carving, wood down by the lakes, or fixing cars, or doing odd jobs, or all the other thousands of things guys in Iowa do when they want to provide for their wife and two children.

Pedro had a great life with a nice family and he looked like a gang member, but did not act or speak like one. These come from nowhere and make good here stories are always inspirational to me, wherever I come across them.

He was on his way to his lawyer's office in Des Moines and with time running out, I knew I would have to do something to get my butt to San Francisco in a hurry. Pirsig or not.

"We're going right by the bus station," he said. And that was that.

Chapter 26

The Bus Stop

Alright, so its not hitchhiking. It's a lot more dangerous.

I knew there was no way I was going to make San Francisco in five days. So when my Honduran/Iowa ride suggested we were close to the Greyhound station, I hopped out.

Des Moines is big and friendly enough, but bus stations are bleak. Des Moines or no.

I'd be in San Francisco in 43 hours. $210.

"I'm hitchhiking across the country and I'm writing a book about it," I told the ticket seller.

"We get a lot of hitchhikers here," he said, pointing to a scruffy, dirty, transparently insane guy that I knew I could smell even though he was still 25 yards away and there was 25 people in between us.

I said a silent prayer that we would not be on the same bus. Or near each other on the same bus. I had to work a bit holding my breathe over the next two days to make that happen.

"When's your book coming out?"

"Not sure, but you can follow it on myspace," and I handed him a card with my address.

A few minutes later I was grabbing a coke about 10 yards away when he yelled over: "Hey man, you're getting on a G-4." He was laughing.

I'd forgotten in addition to my travel pictures, I had some private pictures of good ole Colin boarding and enjoying himself on a private jet. If he said it was a G-4, that was good enough for me.

I've hitchhiked to Vegas. Drove. Flew commercial. Flew first class. And flew in a private jet with drinks and nice clothing.

Believe it or not, every way has its merits. But thinking about flying in private jets put me in a good mood as I got ready for my 43 hour ground flight to San Francisco.

I probably could have or should have flown. But somehow, I thought taking the bus presented the best opportunity for (mis) adventure.

As I hopped on, I wondered why the driver's seat was surrounded by a thick plastic cage like some bullet proof heavy armor. Turns out it was not like some bullet proof heavy armor, it was bullet proof heavy armor.

In a few hours, outside of Rawlings, Montana, where we stopped to pick up a 30-something white guy with a long goatee, shaved head, and a 10-day stubble, I found out why: This bus stopped at prisons.

The con bounded into his seat two rows up from me and announced, "That town sucks, I just got out of prison and couldn't find no drugs in that town no where."

Later I realized Rawlings is where the two kids from Buffalo picked me up on their way to the senior prom, right after the son of the Merry Prankster dropped me off. I wondered about the prom. That seemed a lifetime ago.

"I just did three years. Sale of Meth Am Phet A Meen. It wasn't too bad."

He didn't give off a threatening or violent vibe as much as a novel one. It was more like Kiwanis Club on steroids.

And novel is good on long bus trips.

For the next 24 hours, on the bus and at the rest stops, he kept a running monologue about prison life for several of the passengers. At McDonald's he was talking about a scam to get "green money" into prison that involved some pen pal that would smuggle stuff to him during visiting hours.

Don't ask.

The bus had about 40 passengers, including three women who dressed and act like boys – tough teenage boys -- complete with short hair, tattoos, baggy pants, and the rest. One was sitting in front of me and sucked her thumb most of the way to the West Coast.

"I'm going to San Francisco because I like the water," she told me in an oddly juvenile tone. "Do you know where I should go? I have money. I can afford it." And she started fingering an envelope full of 100-dollar bills.

I did not know. I was going to suggest that most people do not go to San Francisco for the water, but I was not in the business of popping her -- and anyone else's -- dreams. Hell, I didn't know anything about San Francisco anyway. Been there about ten times and never really figured out what the noise was all about.

Later that day she was talking to Prison Boy. He smiled at her and arched his back and reached into his hip pocket to pull out a container of prescription pills.

I had not seen a gleeful look like that since standing by Ambassador and political big wig Robert Strauss at the Del Mar racetrack. "I'm winning my ass off," said the ambassador, grinning. He was just weeks away from embarking on a trip to the Soviet Union to make sure its downfall was not a free fall.

Now I saw that look again as Girl Boy and Prison Boy locked eyes and laughed. The last I saw both of them, they were leaving the Oakland bus station, together.

PRINCE

I forgot Prince comes from Minnesota as well. I guess that means boredom equals desperation equals genius.

Chapter 38

The Zen Coach of Hitchhikers

A zen blessing from the maestro.

We pulled into Denver and hunkered down for a few hours.

"Where can I get some breakfast outside the terminal," I asked the guard.

"Two blocks that way."

As I crossed the street I noticed a Ritz Carlton hotel. I've stayed a total of about 20 nights in the Ritz Carleton, but after pulling an all nighter on a Greyhound bus, my first inclination was not to seek out the closest Ritz Carlton.

It wasn't till I was returning from my dingy diner breakfast that it occurred to me that I could actually go into the Ritz and at least get a decent cup of coffee.

I gave myself the once over. I had stashed my backpack -- good. I felt grungy -- bad. But my clothes were clean and my hair was neat so off I went.

But first I had to take care of a final but critical detail. I needed an attitude adjustment. I had to remember what it was like to go into the Ritz as if I owned the place. I took a deep breath. Straightened up and threw off my Greyhound look.

And headed for the front door with an ease borne of confidence, fake but nonetheless real.

"Good morning, suh, how are you today," said the doorman as he swung into action. He smiled, but I did not look at him any further to see if he was giving me the once over. There would be no betraying and guilty glances during this caper.

"Fine. Fine. Happy to be here," I said in my 'just got out of my Bentley' voice as if I were doing him some favor by pretending to talk to him as I looked ahead to what must have been some very important gathering. He seemed grateful.

After a quick trip to the gift shop and business center to use the computer, I headed into the bathroom for a wash. Hands. Face. Rinse, repeat. Hot and clean. After spending all night shifting in my bus seat, the bathroom water at the Ritz revived me as if I were some cripple throwing off his crutches at Fatima. Halleleluja.

I headed downstairs to the lounge for some coffee. I grabbed a copy of the New York Times and made myself at home in the deep and dark oversized leather chairs. Ahhhh.

An elegant young lady set the coffee in front of me. I uncrossed by cowboy-booted legs and reached for my wallet.

"No charge, sir."

Some day I'll figure out why rich people get so much free stuff, while people at Greyhounds stations pay $10 for a $2 sandwich. But not today. Not now. My coffee was gone and so was my paper, complete with crosswords.

I was getting up to say hello to Laker basketball coach Phil Jackson, who was waiting to be seated, standing all by himself.

Two nights before I watched his Lakers lose to Denver from my Iowa hotel room. That night they would go at it again.

Zen Coach Along the Way.

"Hey coach, '72 Knicks. Big Fan," I said giving him a thumbs up. I was walking slowly and did not intend to stop. Not unless he stopped me.

Which he did. "Cool," he said beaming. He was wearing a flip flops beneath a black warm-up suit with two thick gold stripes going down the arms and legs as if he were some kind of admiral in the Navy of the Los Angeles Lakers.

For those of you who were not present at the lunch room of Salesianum School for Boys in Wilmington Delaware in the early 70's, you should know we talked about one thing more than any other: Who was better: The Lakers or the Knicks?

I was a Knicks fan. Walt Frazier. Willis Reed. Dave Bradley, and coming off the bench, the ungainly Phil Jackson. This was one of those magical teams that transcended the sport.

And today when people in New York say they are Knick fans, most are just yearning for a return to the style and dignity and class and success of this team.

Since then, Phil has won 10 championships as a coach, surpassing Red Auerbach of Celtic fame. I have seen him and his teams hundreds of times over the years, but I always think of him as a Knick.

Phil was not the kind of player to inspire kids on playgrounds. These players, of course, are often the best coaches.

I met Phil's team mate, Bill Bradley, once when he was running for president. "Knick's fan," I mumbled, standing up to shake his hand with all the confidence a shy 15 year old boy could muster meeting his hero. Though of course I was at least 25 years older.

On the playground, I was Bill Bradley whenever I hit a 20 foot shot, which was one of the few things I could do with a basketball.

I tried to sit down but Bradley locked on to me and we started talking about basketball. Fun. For the next month, every time NBC News did a story about the waning fortunes of the Bradley campaign, they would show B roll of Bradley and me talking Knicks B-ball.

I figured hey, if I can talk to the star, I can sure at least say hello to the benchwarmer.

"So what are you doing out here," Phil asked. Somehow he knew the fans of the '72 Knicks were not brewed in the clear mountain water of Denver.

"Hitchhiking around the country, writing a book on it. Staying off the freeways. Hitting the small towns."

He got it: "Pirsig. Zen and the Art of Motorcycle Maintenance," he said smiling, as a couple of guys I would later identify as coaches joined us to whisk him away. I started to pull away.

"Good luck tonite, coach."

And shaking his head with bemusement, the Zen coach pronounced the zen blessing: "You too. Good luck on your journey."

BACK TO PRISON BOY.

I headed back to the Bus stop across the street. That was the longest 100 yards I ever walked. When I finally boarded the bus, Girl Boy was asleep, sucking her thumb. And prison boy was talking about making some money.

Four hours later we were piling out of the bus and into a McDonald's for lunch when I spotted an old and tattered and yellowed copy of Zen and Motorcycle Maintenance on the seat four rows up. It was one of the other Girl Boys, or should it be Boy Girls. This one with heavy tattoos.

A few minutes later I found her outside, smoking a cigarette after a Big Mac. "Hey is that your book, Zen and the Art of Motorcycle Maintenance?"

She was all friendly. "Yeah, but I'm only on page 4. My friend says I have to read it."

"Great book. I've spent the last month running around the country hitchhiking and writing a book about it. Kind of like that book, but less intense. I just saw Phil Jackson, coach of the Lakers in the Denver and we talked about it a bit."

She looked at me as if I were the one dressed like a boy but really a girl. I didn't press it but I thought it was funny, even if it took her a bit to decide whether to believe me or not. I pressed on.

"Pirsig likes motorcycles because it gives you a better quality experience over driving. In a bike you are not hermetically sealed. You are open to all the sounds and smells and experiences that a car shuts out. Whatever biking has over cars, hitchhiking has over biking, only ten times more so."

She nodded, knowing that she would not know what I was talking about a few hours or days. And tossing our remaining Micky D wrappers, we headed back to our hermetically sealed, oversized Pirsig capsule.

In San Francisco, I gratefully grabbed a cheap hotel room and slept, slept, slept. The Big Meeting the Big CEO had with his Big and Indispensable Media Guru was cancelled 'till later in the summer.

It could be a few days. It could be a few weeks. I decided it would have to be a few days 'cause I did not know what I would do it were any further away.

So after a few days, I headed out.

Chapter 26

The Secret of Coffee in Iowa

I was still wondering about Iowa when Frank picked me up as usual in the middle of nowhere.

With a new Buick LeSabre at the end of a day, I was feeling good.

"My wife passed away five years ago and I still miss her," he told me. Frank was in his 80's and heading for Walmart 50 miles away. "We really got along well. Married 50 and a half years."

"What was your secret?"

"If I ever felt myself getting angry with her, I would just say 'honey, I've got some chores to finish up in the basement, where I had woodworking tools.

And I went downstairs to cool off. A little while later she would bring me a cup of coffee and say 'I thought you'd want a cup of coffee."

Now you know.

Chapter 27

Who Turned Off the Mojo?

or Darkness on the Edge of Town.

Ever since I took the bus for a detour in San Francisco, I've been having a hard time getting a ride.

I'm heading up 101, North of San Francisco, hoping for a coast run to the redwoods and maybe Oregon. I get stuck North of San Francisco in Healdsburg. So I'm waiting and waiting; listening to the Lakers playoff game on the radio and grateful that it is on. Radio can be a bit sparse in the early evening and getting a chance to listen former coach Dr. Jack Ramsey is hitting the jackpot.

For the first time, I take out my video camera and start playing with it. Then it strikes me: Hey, I've been out here two hours.

That's too long. So I walk into town, get something to eat and walk to the next entrance. It was dark by the time I found it. And I knew my chances for a ride were not good.

I could see the hotel sign just a few blocks away, but tonite I had another back up plan: tonite I would go hobo. I'll sleep under some trees on the side of the road.

Come 11 O'Clock, I start hunting my spot. All I could see was dark, damp, hard ground with lots of nameless, shapeless small animals crawling around. The grass was waving, so was the trees. Casting shadows, each one with long, sharp teeth.

So I woosed out and hit the hotel. The next day I returned to the same spot. And what the night before looked like the far side of the River Styx, today looked like an amber corner of the Elysian Fields. A meadow.

Last night the shadows held snakes. Today, the big green trees cast beautiful shade that I was almost surprised did not contain a big picnic basket, overflowing with checkered tablecloths, fried chicken and cole slaw. And don't forget the pitcher of lemonade.

I am of course talking about the exact same place through I do not ask you to believe it, because I scarcely do.

Chapter 28

The Twitcher and Me.

I finally got to sleep outside hobo-style the next day in Ukiah, where I had a power nap under an elm tree in the loop on the freeway entrance. Nice.

When I awoke it was supper time and my last ride told me there was a Jack in the Box and a Wal-Mart just across the road. I needed some Rogaine and never could resist a Super Taco so off I went.

After a month on the road, I could not really remember seeing any other hitchhikers. But as I waited for my Jack in the Box tacos, I noticed a young woman talking to herself and walking around.

About every third step her whole body would twitch, hurling her limbs inward.

One thing I notice about Ukiah was lots of cops: Local, county and state. So I had no trouble imagining the cops getting a call about some hitchhiker acting funny near Jack in the Box and them finding me instead, and how I would have to convince them I was not the psychotic twitcher they were after.

That is more difficult than it sounds.

An hour later, I was on the road catching another basketball game on the radio. Except this time the reception was poor, so I had to keep moving my head and body every 30 seconds of so to improve the reception.

You might have actually thought I was twitching.

My next ride took me one mile.

Chapter 29

Colin Fights the Law.

It was a draw.

I could not get out of Ukiah. So finally I just found a light post, sat down, and stuck out my thumb for cars entering the on ramp.

I could almost hear the cars laughing as they passed; looking down on me as I begged for a ride. I was going to sit and just didn't care: I was tired and in no great hurry anyway. I had my radio and my ball game and that was just fine by me.

The game was almost over when two girls, a guy and a dog appeared on my radar screen from some railroad tracks about a quarter of a mile away. As they got closer, it was clear these road warriors were young and probably better described as homeless.

Fellow hitchhikers.

"You hitching too?" they asked. "That's cool."

"Yeah, I'm writing a book about it."

And soon we were sitting at McDonald's, a few blocks away. I was buying them their first meal all day and they were happy and effusive. The guy ordered something from Mikky D's "secret menu."

The two girls, both caked in grime, heavy, and covered in tattoos, one prison style, the other professional. They had a matter of fact air about them. They told me about their life on the road.

Way more grueling than glamorous. A month later they would email me to make sure I knew all about the Burning Man Festival in New Mexico.

The manager waited on us and pretended not to notice the unusually unkempt condition of her newest customers. No they would not be filming a commercial with this crowd. But she smiled at me when I handed her the 20 to pay for 19 dollars worth of food.

I wanted to ask about their parents and family and where were they and all those questions, but I did not. Instead I asked them about hopping trains.

"That's not hard," said the girl without the shock of pink hair on top of an otherwise short almost shaved head. The other two nodded, as if they were wondering how anyone could be confused about something as simple as "train squatting."

"Squatting?"

Fellow Road Warriors

"Yeah, that's what we call it."

That's pretty much what they called everything every time they had to find something to eat or somewhere to sleep.

"Train squatting is not hard, you just find a train, get on it and hide. Then wait."

"How long?"

"Sometimes seven, eight hours."

I was better at hiding than waiting. So I told them "A few weeks ago a railroad engineer told me not to get caught or else the feds would put me in jail for a few days."

But my little observation from tourist land was not what they were talking about.

"That's no problem. You have to hide from the squatters. The other people on the train. Because they will kill you. They will throw you off the train while it is moving."

More head nodding. Dang.

"So if you get on a train and see anyone else on it, get off right away and run."

They went on for a bit about squatting crews and how there were lots of them. All of them dangerous.

I reviewed my list of things to do on the Great Hitchhiking Trip just to make sure that running into roving bands of heavily armed sociopathic teenagers was not on the list.

Copter's a Comin'

That is what I was doing when I was snapped back into reality by Ukiah Guy talking about San Diego. He was a good kid. A good looking kid. He might have had something going on at one time, but there was something missing now and we knew it. So did he. I suspected it was from the head injury in a car accident he had a year ago. He showed us the scars and told us the story.

But now he had something important he needed to say. Something so good it was scarcely believable even to him.

"You can sleep on the doorways in downtown San Diego. I'm not lying. And no one will say a thing about it. I didn't believe it either," he said, looking at the two girls, who were reserving judgment. "But it's true. I was sleeping in a dentist's door for almost a week. In the morning, before the dentist got there, the nurse would walk up to us real quiet and tell us it was 8 0'clock and time to get up. Sometimes she would give us something to eat and some of those small plastic toothbrushes before the dentist got there."

I did not ask the name of the dentist because for some reason I did not want to hear that it was mine. Nor did I tell them about my stint as a city council staffer whose duties included downtown and how to "clean it up" when confronted with street people sleeping in doorways.

This was in the early 80's and downtown San Diego had lots of homeless people sleeping on doorways. And lots of struggling businesses trying to stay open without scary homeless people scaring away scarce customers.

So when Clancy the Cop, a costumed security guard, told me about his plans to dump water on sleeping homeless people, I encouraged him.

Whew: the crap hit the fan after that. We got mugged by every clergy and do-gooder for miles around and Clancy had to stop. The homeless got their doorways back. The people lost their businesses. But no one seemed to want to talk about that.

I probably would have told my new friends about that, except that these kids did not really engage with me or each other unless the topic was food or cigarettes or beer. When anyone talked about anything other than that for more than 45 seconds, they would just turn and walk away, mid-sentence.

Pinkie pulled one of these exact maneuvers: "All I need now is a beer and a cigarette and that will be a perfect end to the day."

I knew my time with them was almost over so I suggested we could make that happen at a convenience store across the street, then I would hit the road again. But before we left I asked them about sleeping. I told them I usually stay at hotels, but that I was thinking about staying outside for a while.

"I don't have a sleeping bag though," I said. "I'm packing kind of light."

"If you want to sleep, you have to have something to wrap around you," said Ukiah Guy. "It's kind of swaddling on a baby. It just helps you get to sleep faster and better."

I found out that was true. A few times.

Soon I was asking one of the girls what kind of cigarettes she wanted when over my shoulder I heard "got some ID?'

She did not. And the clerk explained how he could not sell me the smokes if they were for her. And he knew they were for her because he heard me asking her. Great, the Matlock of Ukiah asking a 25-year old for cigarette ID.

I knew that was not the only place in Ukiah that sold cigarettes so I paid for two cans of beer and handed over them over to my new crew outside the store.

Ukiah Guy started telling me about getting free food from restaurants. "Yeah, sometimes I eat filet mignon every nite from really good restaurants. All you have to do is wait outside, two doors down and when anyone walks by, just ask if you can have their leftovers. Easy."

The girls agreed this was a great thing to do since most people do not even eat their leftovers.

I was tempted to hang out with my new gang and learn about the scam/squatter lifestyle. But I did not want to turn this into a journey of how to travel cheap while on the lam.

We went across the street to get the cigarettes, and I took their pictures –using the snap shot function of my video camera -- while they struck a Charlie's Angels' pose: Fingers stuck in the air, as if they were holding a pistol at the ready.

Ukiah Guy objected at first. Not dignified enough.

We wrapped it up and wished each other luck and safety in our travels. As I headed back to the on ramp, the last I saw of them they were walking across a dim parking lot, not disappearing as much as dissipating.

As I walked past the store where the clerk had refused to sell me cigarettes, a cop car raced by. Followed by a helicopter. I wondered what kind of town Ukiah was that it required so many cops racing to and fro. Then I noticed the clerk, the stereotypical big bellied, middle aged, bearded, sloppy, nerdy guy, complete with a cartoon T-shirt that barely reached his belt was talking to another cop, making loud noises and big gestures.

Helicopters Looking for Dangerous Criminals.

You know of course I'm describing the exact replica of the comic book store guy on the Simpsons.

My cop reporter instincts kicked in: Maybe I'd see some major bust of some major criminal. A little shooting would be fine by me.

From 50 yards away he was looking at me and looked happy. Very happy. All I heard was the word "backpack."

That didn't make any sense. There was no way he could be talking about me or my new crew. I did not have the slightest idea what he was talking about. But I suspected the helicopter was after the same ne'er do well.

A few minutes later I found out who was the object of his enthusiastic discussion with John Law: Me.

Why was this fat dude pushin' me?

The police cruiser pulled himself away from Comic Book Guy and headed my way. He stopped and a young officer got out. He wanted to know if I bought those kids a beer, and if so, why, if they were not old enough to drink.

"They were both 25," I said, referring to the girls. Ukiah Guy did not drink.

"Did you see their ID's?"

"Uh…Uh …no."

"Then how did you know how old they were?"

Guess he had me there. Now I learned a long time ago not to argue with a cop because you can win the battle but not the war. Besides, I'm usually on their side. But not now.

I also remembered my house rules when my kids were younger. If you want to talk back, go ahead. It just better be funny. So I blurted out.

"They looked a lot older than you." And they did. This cop still had the apple cheek thing going on.

I thought it was funny. He did not. I prepared myself for the Ukiah equivalent of sending me kids to the bathroom for 15 minutes – our standard punishment -- the perp walk to the back of the cop car.

As we talked more and more of my answers turned more and more stammer-like. A helicopter – a helicopter! – hovered overhead, and radioed Apple Cheek that he could not find the kids anywhere.

Never had a helicopter chase me and my crew before. Maybe I should get out more.

Apologetic, I was soon on my way.

Twenty minutes later a late model SUV braked to a stop in a dark and dangerous place. A place that was also my only option. I got in and behind us a car honked insistently. Twice.

It was the manager from Micky D's and she was taking me where I wanted to go.

Chapter 30

Dylan Updates Numbers One and Two.

NPR just did a story about a group of 20 people who celebrate Dylan Days – Dylan's birthday – in Northeast India.

Which of course is also where the Dalai Lama is also wildly popular.They sing. They party. They appreciate Dylan "more than they could put into words." Which was OK since they spoke mostly Hindi.

One of the songs was almost a parody, complete with convenience store accent. The other was clear and beautiful and as sweet a rendition of Dylan as I have ever heard.

Dylan Days Update #2.

Dylan's Malibu neighbors are suing him because a porta-potty he keeps for workers on his estate is creating a nuisance. It stinks.

They even tried setting up huge industrial fans to blow the stench the other way. To no avail.

Insert you own punch line here about blowing in the wind.

Soon after, a 21-year old mechanical engineering student – pretty and elegant despite her dirty hands and work clothes -- farm pulled over at the entrance of the organic farm where she worked and hauled me Northward.

The Weed.

"Hi, I'm T.J."

That was an unusual greeting on two counts: Most people wait a spell before introducing themselves, and I had just plopped down in the front seat of his late model Japanese pickup.

And most people don't have nicknames any more.

"Hi, I'm Weed."

I could have said Coley Bay, Little Pot, Slim, or a few other tags I had received over the years. If the people I grew up with had been in the car, they could have introduced themselves as Duck, Little Rick, Poochie, Mysterious Mike, Snake, Hound Dog, Dog, Head, All Star, Duh, Snip, Reds, Pearl, Dandy Lion, and on and on and on.

Now everyone has play dates and proper names, thank you very much.

Chapter 31

What I learned at the marijuana grower's seminar:

Don't call it marijuana. Call it medicine.

Don't let the cops find your guns and cash.

If you have kids, keep them away from the medicine, the processing tables, the drying racks, the scales, the pipes, and other paraphernalia. Especially do not use your child's crib to dry your medicine. Some at Child's Protective Services are not particularly understanding of any of these situations.

No one asked, and no one answered, whether if was OK to smoke, I mean use, medicine in the presence of children. Or whether it was OK for kids to imbibe.

When kids get older, make sure their clothes don't smell of cannabis when they go to school.

Smoking pot makes people talk a very, very, very long time. Especially at seminars with portable microphones. Especially lawyers.

Smoking pot shortens attention spans of people not talking at seminars. Especially lawyers.

Pot growers worry that legalization will open the door for evil corporations to make money off of their holy sacament. If they ever meet a South Dakota farmer, they would know these hard working, no-nonsense growers will be growing the finest dope in the world and selling it at commodity prices within one season of legalization.

When traveling to visit, plan, cultivate, process, sell, use or just talk about your crop of medicine, you'd better disable – better still remove and destroy – all the GPS tracking devices in your car and cell phone.

They can tell.

Marijuana not only cures every disease on earth, it also apparently opens up users to all manner of mystical experiences and earthly delights that the rest of us have yet to discover. Among the items not on that list: Clean fingernails. Hair conditioner. Clothes that fit. And breathing between paragraphs.

They serve really, really good chocolate cookies that disappear really quickly.

They have their own radio station -- KMUD -- that airs two kinds of programs: songs about pot; and talk shows about pot.

When people call it medicine, don't laugh out loud.

Chapter 31

The Pot Seminar: The Rest of the Story

What a field day for the heat.

I had not set out to attend a meeting of the largest growers, users and advocates of marijuana in the largest marijuana growing region of the nation.

A few folks had mentioned the marijuana thing but as I left Fort Bragg and started dialing in my radio while I waited for my next lift, it occurred to me that I was sorry I had not had a chance to see at least some of it.

That changed when even before my radio found a station, Acorn pulled over and waved me in.

"I thought you were a local," he told me a few minutes later. "Your clean and have a small backpack. I pick up hitchhikers all the time. They are usually dirty and hungry and smell bad. I call'em road toads."

"I think I met a few of them last night. Two girls and a guy."

"They usually have a dog."

True that.

Acorn was on his way to a meeting. The meeting started one hour ago, and it would take us one hour to get there. He invited me along and of course I thought that sounded like fun.

Pretty soon Acorn was doing his Formula One shifting up and down through some of the tightest turns and smallest roads overhanging a mountain hundreds of feet over the clouds. All the while passing "tourists" and smoking … well you know what he was smoking.

"You want some?" he asked.

"That's Ok."

His girlfriend called. "I just picked up a hitchhiker. He stays in hotels and has credit cards."

They laughed and lost the connection.

Soon we were passing the Grateful Dead farm as well as property owned by Wavy Gravy of Ken Kesey fame. Meeting the guy from Colorado who knew that bunch when he was a kid seemed like a very long time ago.

"Hey Acorn, mind if I take your picture?" I asked as we got closer to the meeting.

"No man, I'm like the Rastas who don't like their picture taken 'cause they believe it takes a little bit of their soul."

That was bullshit. I knew it. He knew it. He knew I knew it. He was paranoid. In his mind, I knew there was a chance that, probably because I didn't smoke, I was some kind of clever DEA agent who wormed his way into his car and into this public meeting.

Now you know why some people don't smoke pot.

Soon we pulled up to a restaurant called Area 101, which apparently is Ground Zero for California's $14 billion a year pot business, mixed in with liberal amounts of conspiracy theory, enviro politics, and alien culture.

At the seminar, a few lawyers and activists answered questions to 40 or so growers, users, and onlookers who sat on plastic chairs and comfortable oversized couches.

Whew, these people could talk and talk and talk. But the people in the audience looked as if they had some money.

Acorn's questions was succinct and passionate and even coherent – much more so than any other I'd heard. Which made me wonder about the quality and quantity of the medicine they were using.

The seminar ended when the panelists were too exhausted to talk and the audience too dazed to listen.

Afterwards, they were smoking a lot of what you would expect them to smoke. Acorn's girl had arrived and though he was a bit standoffish to me during the seminar, we were chatting like old buddies by the time his girl and I figured we came from the same part of the world.

She was bright and attractive and smart and I accepted when they offered to take me 25 miles or so to the north through the Redwoods before they returned to the coast.

"Sorry man, I thought you might have been DEA."

"No problem. I stopped smoking pot when I was 19," I told Acorn's girl in the back seat, a practicing family therapist. "I didn't like the way it made me feel."

"Paranoid?" she suggested.

"Yeah."

"That happens to people who like boundaries."

I asked her about pot. And what police attitudes were up here towards growers and users with kids. "Do you think kids should smoke it?"

"I think everyone should," she said. "It's good for anxiety."

They asked about my family and my travels. And I asked about theirs. "My son is waiting to meet us up the road," she said. "He just got out of rehab for drugs. But he still drinks."

It was not Mr. Strange Hitchhiker's job to confront people with crazy ironies in their lives. Like parents who smoke pot non-stop and wonder why their kids are in rehab. I was dying to know. But I did not ask and I know it did not occur to them to answer. Or even think of the question.

Boundaries.

Soon we arrived at their turnoff. I tool some pictures. We hugged. And they were on their way.

Chapter 32

Ukiah, the sequel.

I was glad to get out of Ukiah, mostly because Ukiah was happy to get rid of me.

They see a lot of hitchhikers there and did not really care for them. I could not really blame them. I would take me a few days to figure out why.

After McDonald's lady dropped me off -- need I say in the middle of nowhere with no lights and no one around? -- I was happy to be on my way out of Ukiah and on my way to the coast.

But it was after midnight. And unless something drastic happened, this might be the night I fulfilled every (else's) hobo fantasies and slept on the side of the road.

My own fantasies still ran to Asian girls and plush RV's.

SAN FRANCISCO TO WILLITS

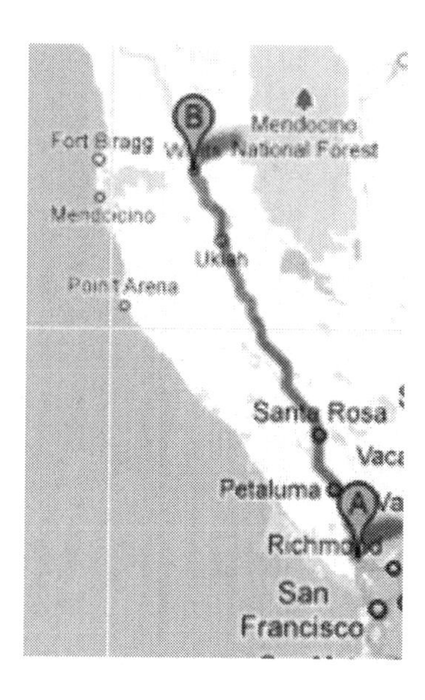

I started praying for a ride. I started Christian, then went Jewish, Islamic, Buddhist, all without result. Then I hit the Roman and Greeks: Zeus, Hera, Thor, and more. Then I hit the obscure ones, ending with Zoroaster.

The last thing I remember before giving up was this message: Zoroaster will not be mocked.

An hour later I was so tired, I gave it a go: I stretched out in a patch of grass near the entrance to the freeway. And I slept for about an hour -- not before seeing a weird green streak of light like a shooting star – but thicker -- that would be of great interest to some folks in a few days.

I slept. When I opened my eyes I knew I wasn't going back to sleep for a while, so I stuck my thumb out. My feet were hurting from my totally good looking but totally non-functioning cowboy boots. So I took them off and stashed them behind my pack.

Which I knew would be a guarantee that soon a cop would pull up.

Sure enough 15 minutes later, a bright light was shining in my face and I was starting my spiel. This time groggy and shoeless on a major road.

"Take your hands out of your pockets," one said. "And where are your shoes?"

I pointed to my pack and put my hands back in my pockets. It was cold and late and that is where they wanted to be.

"TAKE YOU HANDS OUT OF YOUR POCKETS. Don't make me tell you again."

Oh jeez. At least these two Highway patrolmen had the decency to make me put my hands behind my head and lock my fingers together while they searched me, befitting my status as a potentially dangerous criminal of international proportions. At this point, I thought they were overreacting because they had nothing better to do.

In a few days, I would find out how wrong –and stupid – I was.

Soon enough, I was in the car.

"Sorry, pardner, we gotta take you back to the truck stop in Ukiah."

Nooooooooooooooooooooooooooooooooooooooo.

UKIAH, THE SEQUEL 2.

The helicopter and the cops never found my buddies, so they tell me in an email three weeks later.

Chapter 33

The Invasion of Fort Bragg

It may have been cold and late. But I had started my vagabond thing and I was determined to finish it.

So I found a place to sleep. And no, it did not have HBO, free wireless, continental breakfast, and nice clean sheets on a big soft bed.

At 4:30 (a.m. dammit) a faint blue light flickered in the east. It occurred to me that I was breaking one of my most sacred rules: If I was up at dawn, I'd better be having a really really really great time.

Willits to Fort Bragg

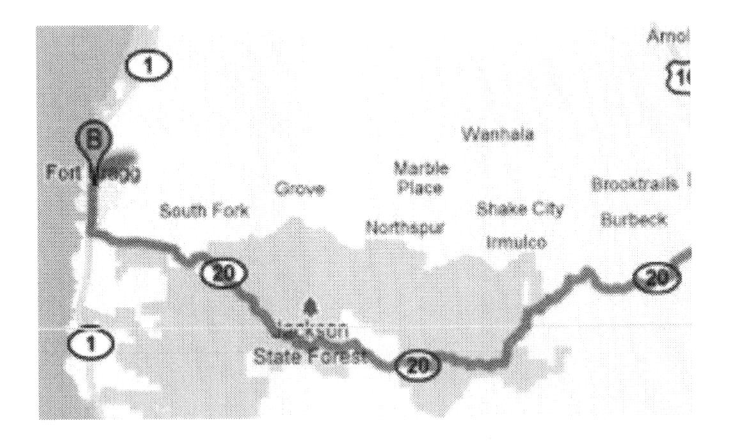

I was cold and tired and uncomfortable, so I wasn't.

As soon as it was bright enough to see my own thumb, I rolled over, walked a few steps, and stuck out my arm. Less than five minutes later I was on my way out of Ukiah, again, this time in a late model luxury KIA.

Warm and soft and safe. God I was grateful.

"I've been getting up at 4 a.m. my whole life," said my spry 89 year old benefactor. "I eyed you pretty good before I stopped. I knew you were OK."

For 30 miles we talked about his family, his time at Wal-Mart, his life as a mechanic, and how he joined the Army while his friend joined the Navy, both winding up at Pearl Harbor, December 7, 1941.

"We figured we were safe and that the war would never reach us way out there," he said. "He's still there on the Arizona."

A few minutes later he pointed to a neat and clean trailer park. "That's where I live but I'll take you up the road where you can catch a ride over to the coast."

About half the time I leave a car, I am in awe of the people who just dropped me off. Old Army Guy was right at the top of that list.

By the time my thumb was out again, it was 6 a.m. and 50 yards away, across the street, 2 guys and a girl and dog were stirring from the blankets spread out in the park.

A few minutes later two more hitchhikers appeared. Or should I say three: A girl, a guy and a dog. They must be getting these kids from central casting.

The girl greeted me as she headed over to Jack in the Box for some coffee. "You hitchhiking too? That's cool."

"Thanks, where you headed?"

"Don't know man."

Had Old Army Guy -- my last ride -- been there, I know he would have started singing that that military marching song: 'you never know where you're goin' till you get there..."

Down the street a park worker turns on the sprinklers. He seems surprised when they rise up and start shouting at him.

With my radio firmly plugged in, and morning talk in both my ears, it was a quick 90 minutes before Noelle stopped and waved me in. She was going all the way to the coast. Fort Bragg. About an hour away.

Finally, my escape from 101 was complete.

She was smart and good looking and until a year before, a reporter at an East Coast radio station. And looney as a looney tune. That's probably not fair to say that. I was happy to be there. But she was. But between the Illuminati, aliens, media conspiracies and pot, pot and more pot, I couldn't tell if I was hitchhiking or sitting through a dry run of the best of Art Bell radio show.

"You ever listen to Art Bell?" I asked, referring to the radio show that popularized all manner of weird and alien things. "You could do that kind of show."

"No, but lots of people tell me that."

"It's a compliment."

I asked her about all the kids hitchhiking. "They come out here in droves to work in the pot farms," she said.

Oh, that's where we were. Pot City USA. I had not known. Even when I thought I knew, I still didn't.

"Could you pass me that black cannister." And with hand on the wheel, she opened it, extracted a joint, lit it, and offered it to me as we weaved in and out of the first of the Redwood forests.

"That's Ok."

"They fired me from a radio station when they told me I wasn't allowed to report the truth. They said I was entertainment. Not news. They would not let me tell the people that Bush stole the election."

By this time, we were cruising through a patch of redwoods, going up and down and around and around the roads with no shoulders -- with apparent ease.

Bush is part of Illuminati, she told me, which I knew to be some kind of ancient conspiracy slash cult.

One minute Bush is an idiot. The next he is an all seeing genius. I wish these folks would make up their minds.

Noelle might be beautiful and stoned, but she is also coherent and articulate and liked to talk. I interrupted her, with apologies beforehand.

"You know you would be good as a radio talk show host," I said. "Most of the liberals on talk radio are dull and humorless. If not a talk show, a podcast. You're a lot better than most of the folks on Air America," the current basement for the liberal radio personalities.

I personally will believe in the Illuminati before I believe that higher taxes and more regulations create jobs. She was a lot further along the sanity spectrum than most leftie radio talkers.

She was all for it but there was that problem with the government following her around and stealing her computer and making sure that she did not get access to the airwaves to tell the truth.

Oh jeez. She handed me her card. "Massage Therapy."

Understatements on the Road.

"I had a girlfriend named Noelle. Trouble. Nothing but trouble. But I sure liked her for a while."

I just checked: The Guinness Book of World Records is officially listing that as the world record understatement for 2009.

We pulled into Fort Bragg. It was cold and cloudy. She parked at the school where she was learning to become a Vegan chef. I thanked her and walked away. Still kind of groggy from not getting much sleep the night before, but energized from spending time with two bright and energetic souls, albeit different.

"Hey," she yelled.

I looked over. She was smiling.

"What did you say your name was?"

What Happens When You Stumble on a Pot Farm

As I edit this, I read in the newspaper a city councilman in Fort Bragg got killed after stumbling on a pot farm.

Chapter 34

The reason there are no gay guys in North Dakota.

I went down my "intimate partner" deal-breaker, must-have checklist:

Dark, almond-shaped eyes?

No.

Soft yellow skin?

No.

Vagina?

No.

Dang. Since John was pretty much going 0-3, I guess I would have to pass on his offer to give me oral sex right before we pulled into the grove of Redwood Trees on the Avenue of the Giants.

Sorry. But no thanks. But Good luck."

He sped off leaving me alone in the first grove of Redwood trees I had ever seen close up.

I knew what I had to do: Walk.

After a half hour it dawned on me why John had dropped me off there: it had lots of nooks and crannies. And that is what he did: Picked up hitchhikers in the hope of a tree-lined and anonymous sexual encounter.

Now I know why there are no gay guys in North Dakota: No trees.

Chapter 35
Walkin' to Weott

The first time I saw a Redwood, I was in a car. I knew I would have to walk among them to see what they were all about.

Zen and the art of all that good stuff.

So after John dropped me off, I headed North. Sometimes on a trail. Sometimes on the road.

It was a weekend day near the end of May and I was kind of surprised at how few people were there.

12 miles later, I was still trying to figure out what to make of those crazy trees.

Still am.

And I will not trivialize it or them by repeating all the cliched comparisons.

But I will say this: It was worth every step.

Come dusk, the park police drove by and suggested it was time for me to camp or make my way to the freeway, two miles away.

As for sleeping in the woods, I should not even think about that.

Which of course was my intention. I had not realized I had become so transparent from so far away.

The ground beneath the redwoods was soft and warm and inviting and perfect for sleeping. But I did not want to disturb the mojo of the primeval forest by dodging cops all night.

I turned at the telephone pole outside of Weott. 33 feet above the ground a sign marked the spot where flood waters rose as they wiped out the town in the 30's. Sorry about that.

FORT BRAGG TO EUREKA

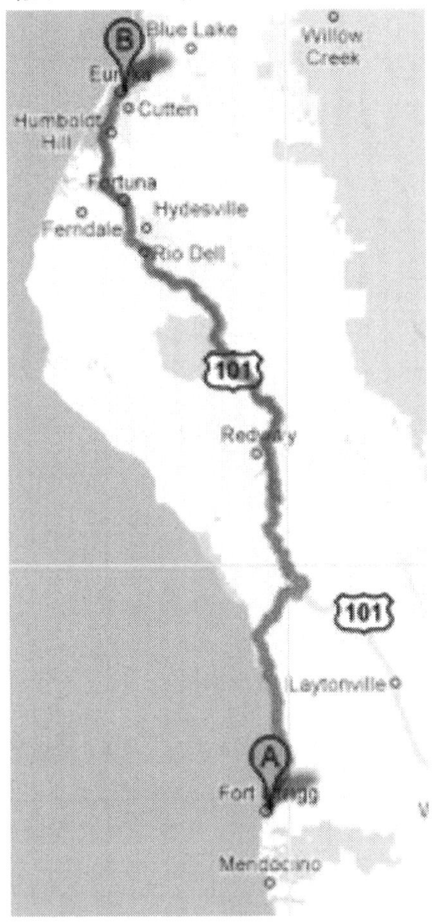

On my way out of the magical forest, I walked up a long hill and approached a stand of a dozen or so houses. The new town of Weott built far above the old.

A dog barked from the sidewalk, so 75 yards down the street, I walked down the middle of the road. The dog, a pit bull mix, eyed me all the way and I knew it was not over.

Its owner, a frumpy woman in a housecoat, came outside. "Frisky, come here. Come. Here."

I still knew it was not over. I kept my eyes forward but my attention on Frisky. I know what it means to send 'fear' vibrations to a a dog. This I was not doing. But from ten yards away, Frisky lunged.

I turned and raised my arm, as if I had a rock, stopping Frisky in his tracks before he returned to Frumpy.

On the porch she stood, with no glance of apology. Or anything. Maybe it was some lingering paranoia from when I was a pot smoking 19 year old punk, but I knew right then that my little scary encounter would provide an evening entertainment for the forest dwellers that night.

The same paranoia that made me see what Frisky was going to do yards before he did it.

I wondered what good it did to live in such a beautiful place if it harbored such ugly people. That would not be the last time I thought that over the next two days.

A few days later, I would come not to blame her one bit and wonder why she didn't have a few more dogs and a gun.

Chapter 36
The Rules

If you have not noticed, I'm skipping around in time a bit.

Don't worry. I just checked the Official Hitch Hikers Guide for Writing about Your Experiences on the Road.

They said it was OK.

Chapter 37

Back through the Redwoods.

Just to remind you, the several hundred mile stretch of land north, east and west of San Francisco is one huge pot farm.

On the way out of Eureka, two experienced hitchhikers stopped and gave me a great ride. Dave told about how to hitch a train and said don't pay any attention to those kids who said people get killed.

"Hey can I take your picture?" I asked as I grabbed my pack from the back of his pickup.

"Take his instead," he said, pointing to his buddy who had been riding shotgun.

He was all for it. "But wait, let me show you something first." And he opened up a big plastic bin full of marijuana plants in full bloom.

Then he smiled, put down the lid; I took his picture and off they went. Into the wild high yonder.

Chapter 38

Partying with Sal

The cage fighter.

I was not out of the magical forest for more than five minutes when Sal pulled over.

A Domer," I exclaimed as I spotted the Notre Dame hat and paraphernalia in his car.

"No, but I always wanted to be."

We talked about Eureka, where I was headed about an hour away. "This is a strange town," he said. "Some of my friends think it is a vampire town."

And soon I could see why: the place was a bit spooky in places where it should not have been. I would soon figure out that growing and using lots of illegal drugs does that to a town. A region. A state.

Sal was a kick boxer, and had just competed in a cage match at the local casino. He was so bright and young and articulate about fighting I tried to convince him that was his future. Not the fighting. The talking.

"You ought to come by my gym tomorrow and say hello," he said. Sounded good.

The next day, I stuck my nose up the window of Sal's gym in downtown Eureka. There were about ten people rolling on the floor, choking each other. Sal was there.

But when I came back an hour later, the gym was dark. Sal was gone. And so was I.

I looked North to Oregon. I wanted to go there to see Jack Godfrey, another of my brother's buddies who were with him when he died, but I was starting to run low on cash and thought I still might want to hover around San Francisco.

I sent him an email saying I would have to postpone our meeting, and I think he might have been kind of relieved. He did not really know what the hell I was doing up there, hitching around, any more than I pretended to know. I think some of the guys who came back have survivor guilt over the guys who did not. Which they should not.

I met him later, and of course I was wrong. He was great.

Chapter 39

Colin and the Psycho.

or Colin Almost Gets Killed -- because saying murdered sounds too dramatic.

"What kind of pot do you want?"

One minute before Peter the Jeweler picked me in Garberville, Ground Zero for California's $14 billion pot crop, I was listening to the pot industry's very own radio station, KMUD. It was 7:05 p.m. and time for the "Environmental Hour."

"I was on the river last weekend and boy the water level is dropping. I know because I put some beers in the river to get cold before I went to sleep and when I awoke, the beers were totally out of the water. We all know why: It's because everyone up here grows pot and is using all the water."

O.K. then.

I was making my way down from Eureka. My last ride was a couple of youngish guys whose parting words were "hey, check out the bin in the back." So he lifted it up the lid to show me a bunch of marijuana plants. I figured out they had grown them from seeds and were now delivering them to eager customers throughout Garberville.

Specialization and all that.

I had stumbled around the fringe of the cons, criminals and hippies who had turned this remnant of the counterculture into a vast criminal conspiracy. Or religious movement if the spirit so moves you.

I was regretting that for all the talk, I would not see the real thing. I was a) Wrong. B) Very, very stupid.

That's when Peter Cartier, "like the Jeweler," showed up.

Peter the Psycho

"Don't worry about the dog," he said, pointing to his lab, pit bull mix. "She attacks on my command and she doesn't like people but she seems to like you."

Dogs were no problem for me. Never were. I like them and they like me.

Peter the Jeweler had the bearing and uniform of the aging hippie grower/user/hustler. Dog. Beat-up pickup. Scruffy look. A free but useful spirit who had found his way on his own terms in this world.

Add friendly and 'wired to the gills' to the mix and that was Peter the Jeweler. So I thought.

"People say I'm a little intense. But I've always been that way."

And for the next 15 miles, Peter talked almost non-stop about his 1 ½ years in prison; his return to jail the next month for blowing a .28 DUI; his plants; his life as a petty and not so petty criminal in Detroit.

I told him about my little adventure at the pot growers' seminar.

"I grow some weed. No big deal. As long as you have under a hundred plants, nobody bothers you out here."

That did not count the Mexican cartel of course. They get blamed for bothering a lot of things. If someone leaves town and doesn't let anyone know, it's the cartel. When I stayed in Garberville on the way North a few days before, a warning about the cartel was part of the hotel's welcome package.

"If you take that highway, don't go off the road," she said pointing to the map. "That's where the cartel is and they will kill you."

Fair enough.

I did not plan on running into any hyper-violent dope growers or dealers. Besides, how dangerous could these hippies up here really be?

So I was thoroughly entertained by Peter the Jeweler by the time he dropped me off in the middle of the Redwood forest near a grove with a house made from a single log.

It was so nice and pleasant that I was actually hoping no one would pick me up so I could sleep among the giant trees. Swaddling blanket or not.

I gave Peter the Jeweler my card and took his picture.

"Hey man, write down my number in case you need it. And here's my cell too. Call if you have any trouble."

Sure enough, though my phone was still sitting at the Northeastern Crossroads of Iowa.

We shook hands, I petted his dog, and he was gone with a smile on his face. Mine too: I basked in glow of a good ride from an interesting person in a great part of the world as I geared up for my next ride; i.e. getting the radio ready, putting on my shades, finding a comfortable place to stand.

Five minutes later, Peter was back.

"Hey man, I was thinking, do you need a place to stay tonight? I got a couch"

"No, no thanks."

Then he said the magic words: "Come on, I'll show you what a real pot farm looks like. Get in."

Now that sounded interesting. I did not have any interest in smoking or growing or anything like that. But if I could find a bunch of hippies beating the man at his own game, I thought that would be interesting.

Stupidity was in the air.

Soon we were off the main road; off the side roads, and barreling through a maze of dirt and stone roads.

"Hey man, I'm not gay or anything like that," he said. "I jack off once in a while."

It was this odd admission that set the first of my klaxons ringing.

He restarted his verbal jag: Life in Detroit, growing up in a boy's home orphanage, working for mafia as a drug mule, driving a cab for 14 years, working construction, running strip clubs, moving to Mendo County, how he was a full blown Detroit hippy but no one cared because the other growers did not like him.

"I'm from Detroit man. These people out here are stuck up." Then he took off his sun glasses and for the first time I looked into his eyes. This guy was crazy on some deep level. I just didn't have the smarts to know which level that might be.

Meanwhile, he kept talking. Detroit. Mitch Ryder. Iggy Pop and the Stooges. John Lennon. And drugs, drugs, drugs.

It didn't add up, but I wasn't counting. But soon enough it was clear enough: This guy not just a harmless hippy pot grower, but I did not know what.

I did not feel threatened but I did think it strange when he repeated the "I'm not gay," mantra three or four times before we reached his locked gate.

Klang. Klang Klang.

Soon we were in his yard and hundreds of pot plants waved in the evening breeze. He gave me "the tour," all the while oddly inappropriate comments about sex were coming every few minutes. Three girls were supposed to come over that night, but "they through."

Something inside me said 'take a picture now," but I did not.

I looked him over and the thing that seemed an eccentricity 30 minutes before now glared red at me: His sneakers. Below a tattered t-shirt and cargo short pants he sported a brand new pair of Van skateboard sneakers, complete with thick new laces.

Whenever I see an older guy adopting the dress and manner and of teen and pre-teen boys, I get the heeby jeebies. I assume the guy is some kind of pedophile or other kind of gay freak.

Still I did not feel threatened. But it was clear that something was going on other than the dog and pony show hippie boy was putting on for me.

"Hey man, great to have you here. I get lonely up here. People don't have compassion anymore, man. We need more of that … Me man, I feel destined for something. Something great. I've always felt that way. Something great."

"Happy to be here," I said as he went back to his bound for greatness and compassionate rant.

By this time, I still believed there was a chance that I could stay for a few days and see a real part farm in action complete with all the people building fences, planting new crops, tending to the old ones.

I still believed there was a chance I was wrong about this guy. That he could be at least partly sane. But he never seemed dangerous. That means there were two of us with delusions.

Soon we were inside his "cabin." I noted, with no interest, a collection of knives, a crossbow, and other weapons mounted on the wall near his door. Ornaments. That's all they were, ornaments.

The cabin was a dark, two story dump with a goodwill couch in front of a later model TV. Soon we were upstairs in his room on the tour.

"You stay there tonight," he said, pointing at another goodwill couch next to his poster bed. I knew by then there was no chance of that, though I did not say so.

Out of the closet came a box. Out of the box came bags and bags of dope of all sizes and shapes. From buds and leaves all the way to powder. Big bags.

He opened each and offered it up to my nose for inspection. Smelly bags.

I recognized the smell right away: It was the same smell that had been oozing from every pore in his body. I gave a perfunctory 'hmmm' but told him I had no idea what I was seeing or smelling.

"That OK, man, I could write a book on this shit."

Then came the pictures of old girl friends. "She was Miss Michigan in 1984," he said. "Went out with her for two years." The picture was a worn and canned head shot without a name or anything else except for a few stains that could have come from a beer, or more likely, a bong.

We went downstairs and for some reason I thought we'd go outside, it being right in the middle of the redwoods and the weather being so nice and all.

But instead we plunked down on the couch in the dark living room and the smoking started. He offered me some.

"That's OK," I told him. But after spending almost a week around people who thought marijuana was some kind of sacrament, I do admit I was curious about re-examining my long held beliefs that I did not really care for the stuff.

I did know that if I stayed there I'd probably get a contact high. And soon I did, complete with all the vivid sounds from the TV and a pleasant feeling of heaviness.

The smoking stopped but the talking continued, high gear. I pitched in once in a while just to let him know I was listening.

There were more stories: Motorcycle gangs and money; Detroit rock stars like Mitch Ryder and Iggy Pop. "I get lonely up here man, thanks for coming."

All of a sudden he was in the middle of his couch, just a foot or so away from me, if that. Klang. Klang. Klang.

"You like Root Beer floats?"

"How about a shower?"

"You want to take some weed with you tomorrow?"

"I'll give you a lift to Ukiah."

"And by the way, I'd prefer it if you don't sleep on this couch tonight. Use the one upstairs."

I'm small, but I can bench 350 pounds. Here, feel my arms." And he flexed and held his forearm out in front of me.

I made a fist and punched it lightly. "Tight," I said. I knew it was getting weird.

By now he had switched the TV to the terrified teenager fare of Chiller Theater. The Playboy Channel was no where to be found. The only conceivable interest I had expressed in it was telling him I was not gay but did not care if anyone else was.

He made two phone calls and left two messages after no one answered. One to a landlord, the other to a girl.

By then it as dark out and the only light we had was the TV. "Hey man, you don't mind if I try some of this, do you?" And he pulled out a small glassine bag with white powder along with a small glass pipe.

"I figure if I use just so much of it a day, this will last till I have to go to jail next month," he said.

I'm not a drug expert, so I do not know whether it was coke or meth or crack or whatever. But I was sure it was a big bag of crazy that this guy did not need. Nor did I.

By this time I knew I was going to slip away as soon as Dr. Hippiestein called it a night. I guessed that before then, I would have to tell him I wasn't buying whatever he was selling. I thought it was going to be some kind of weird gay thing.

I was disappointed there would be no behind the scenes look at Captain Kangaroo's harmless hippy pot farm.

"Hey man, let me see if I can do something about the electricity," and he started poking around the fuse box with a screw driver. For some reason, a guy smoking crack and poking around a fuse box did not seem that strange. Some girl was screaming on the TV.

I was just sitting on the couch waiting to see what crazy thing would happen next.

He shut the front door, using his shoulder to bang it twice. Then he locked it, saying "I'm going to lock it just in case the landlord comes by."

But that was a lie. I knew it. And that set off a full Klaxon alarm.

Had he not told me, I would not have noticed that he locked it. I did not know what he was up to, but I was alarmed and I would not be locked in with Peter the Jeweler.

No. No. No.

I told him I did not feel comfortable with that door locked. "So please open it."

He pretended not to hear me, then he reached for a bayonet on his wall.

Hatchet? I'm Not Cool With Hatchets.

Everything fell away all at once: All of his hippy bullshit. All of his "I'm just another girl lovin' guy' talk; all of his fake calls to the landlord and girlfriend; the bogus pictures of the bogus girlfriend. And what was left in that moment was a convict high on crack coming at me with a bayonet.

Everything slowed down. Way down.

This was ten steps past alarmed: This was get scared and get ready to fight for your life time.

"Did I tell you I like weapons?" And he held the bayonet out to me.

I took it, handed it back and asked him to open the door again. If it seems stupid to you that I actually handed the knife back, imagine how stupid it feels to me now, writing about it.

There's no etiquette for knife handling with crack fiends.

"Hey check this out," and pulled a curved knife off the wall. "Feel the blade. Sharp as a razor."

I did. It was. "Yeah, that's sharp. Now open the door."

He replaced the curved razor picked up a hatchet. He removed the leather cover and ran his fingers over the edge and side of the blade as if he were caressing it as he looked at me, then back to the blade.

No one talked.

"Hey man, you don't have to worry about me, I'm harmless," he grinned. There was no doubt in my mind I was looking into the mind and heart and eyes of a very sick and dangerous person.

"Open the door."

If he lunged, I would be ready. I was turned sideways, a classic martial arts defensive pose I first learned from my old college roommate Jimmy. I thought about the classic defense of the unarmed man against an attacker with a knife: Use the forearm, no matter how much it hurts. No how much it gets shredded. Sacrifice the forearm to fend off the blade.

I got ready.

"Hey man, you don't have to be intimidated by me."

"I'm not afraid of you," I said immediately. I heard my own voice, slow and deep and serious. "I just don't like your weapons."

He put the hatchet back on the wall and opened the door. I walked through it.

Outside he apologized profusely. He invited me back in. I knew there was no way I was going back in that house. I grabbed my bag, took out my sweater and put it on. "Thanks for showing me around," I said. I thought it was important to let him know I was at least pretending not to care about whatever he was going to try and do to me. That I could handle it.

"Oh man, you're not going are you? I was just having a little fun. Come on, put your pack up in my room."

That's how whacked he was: He thought I was actually going to do that.

"Hey man, don't mind me. I just always had knives growing up in Detroit in boarding school and in high school. It was 97 percent black. Come on man, don't go. Put your pack upstairs."

I knew I was going but I did not want to hurry. Even so, I was not going to stick around and sort out his non-sequitirs. "I'm taking off."

He walked me the 50 yards to his gate, all the while begging me to stay. I walked past a gap in his fence and turned to hear him say: "Hey man, if you go to Detroit, let me know, I'll hook you up."

FIGHT OR FLIGHT TO TAHOE.

My flight or fight response fully engaged, I felt my adrenaline buzz subside as I made my way through the Redwood forest at 11 p.m. Lots of shadows and noises had my full attention.

I was spooked. With downhill my only direction, I made my way back to the road. Two hours and five miles later, I was back on the cold and dark road in, you guessed it, the middle of absolutely no where.

Chapter 40
The Great Escape
Little bit of luck goes a long, long way.

After walking through the dark Redwood forest, I ended up back on Highway 101. It was past midnite, and very cold.

There were no cars coming in either direction, so I sat down and hoped I could get some sleep.

No such luck. It was way too cold.

At 1 a.m. I knew I had to walk just to warm up. I knew there was no chance anyone would stop for me in the middle of nowhere.

But after walking for five minutes, a saw the lights of a car behind me as it lit the highway signs in front of me. I stuck out my thumb. I did not even turn around.

He stopped -- taking about a quarter of mile after jamming on his breaks. "Almost didn't see you."

I did not mention my life threatening incident of a few hours before. By now I had learned that bringing bad vibes into a car was not something that made for good rides. But Tree Man did tell me about Pot Land.

"I used to trim the trees away from the electric lines up here. And most of the time when I knocked at the gates, they were locked. The owners would come out to take me on their property holding a gun. I remember one guy saying 'you didn't see anything up here, right?' I said right, ignoring a few thousand pot plants below my ladder.

"One guy did not let us on his property. I said I'd have to come back the next day with the sheriff. He said he didn't care. The next day we came back and they arrested him for having 500 plants. Stupid."

In pot country, some folks still think the only distinction between pot growers is smart and dumb. They are not in safe or dangerous territory. Not yet.

He took me 250 miles to Placerville, 60 miles or so from Tahoe. "My step son just got out of jail and I'm going to pick him up," said Tree Man.

We ate breakfast and looked for his son. He offered to take me the edge of town and send me on my way.

"I'm not leaving till this mission is accomplished," I told him. An few hours after sunup, a happy looking young guy walked up the truck. I was expecting a loser/jailbird, but I got the opposite. I said hello to one, goodbye to the other and I was on my way.

"Hey can we take you anywhere?"

"No, thanks."

I hopped on a city bus to the outside of town, met a few folks, took some pictures, stuck out my thumb, and ten minutes later a guy did a U-Turn, came back, and took me 250 miles to Placerville, 60 miles or so from Tahoe.

I put out my thumb. Ten minutes later I saw someone else do a U-turn and come back for me. And hour later he had dropped me off in front of the Harrah's in Tahoe.

I got a free room, and was soon asleep.

They go together.

Chapter 41

God that room felt good.

Hello and goodbye to Tahoe.

For some reason the folks at Harrah's in Tahoe declined the opportunity to let me stay at their hotel for five more nights for free. I'd have to go to Vegas for that.

So I'm headed west and south, in a late model pickup, in the company of a former staffer for Governor Pete Wilson of California. We knew a bunch of people in common in San Diego and talked a lot about golf.

He took me way out of his way to get me on the road to Vegas. "Hey isn't the Ponderosa around here?" I asked.

"Eight miles that way," said Wilson Man. "You should check it out."

But exploring the piney ranch of Ben and Hoss and Little Joe Cartwright lost out to the pull of an extended free stay in Las

Vegas, so in the early June sun of the Nevada desert, I stuck out my thumb. Thankful this was one of the cooler summers in memory.

Soon I was driving by small Nevada towns and abandoned copper mines in the company of a well groomed and well spoken guy who seemed polite and happy to have me. After about ten minutes he dropped the big one: "The doctors say I hear voices. And the voices tell me to hurt people. Though I never have and don't want to. So I take pills and they go away."

He could have been telling me what grade of gasoline he used in his big and quiet and late model pickup. He had my full attention for about 30 seconds, then I relaxed.

"Well you know the old saying," I said with an informality I did not really feel, "If you talk to God, they call that praying. If God talks to you, they say you are crazy."

Hitchhiker SuperTherapist. That's me.

Close to 40, he was a high school football star and something of a small town scamp. But now driving between the two Nevada small towns where he lived and his doctor practiced, he felt kind of lost. But oddly happy.

I took his picture and he wrote down the name of his high school football buddy who lived a bit down the road. "If you go by there, look him and tell him I sent you."

"Sounds good."

I took his picture, shook his hand, and said goodbye to the friendliest and nicest person I had met on this trip so far.

Chapter 42

Colin Gets A Gun in Indian Territory.

I ran through my mental checklist to see if I should spend the night at Wes's house:

Did I know him for less than a half hour?

Yes.

Would there be plenty of guns and knives and other weapons about?

Yes, again.

Did Wes live in a hot bed of drugs, alcohol and violence?

Absolutely.

Did he drive a Cadillac?

Sure, an old beat up one. The best kind.

So that settled it. I'd have to give it a go.

Wes was an American Indian, Paute out of North Nevada. I was a couple of hours outside of Tahoe heading to Vegas. I had just posted my Mendo psycho blog on a computer at the local library less than 36 hours after the encounter that scared the piss out of me.

Thirty minutes later I was pushing the debris to the middle of the seat as I settled into the Cadillac.

"Hey Wes, the guy who just dropped me off said Crazy Horse's witch doctor or medicine man or whatever, used to live in these parts. The guy who cast a spell on Crazy Horse that was supposed to make him invulnerable to bullets."

I had visited Crazy Horse memorial in South Dakota, though I still had not written about it.

Wes was all over that.

"That's true. But his wife used a metal spoon to make his meal and that ruined the Ghost spell and that was why he got shot."

He also talked lots about Indian women "on their monthlies," but I did not quite get that.

Wes was a hunter, a philosopher and a naturalist – and had the skins to prove it. And that night, Wes wanted to take me hunting.

Soon we were at Wes's house on the reservation. His pretty girlfriend Elizabeth greeted us while a passel of kids ran around.

In the backyard, several skins soaked in 10 gallon buckets of water ("no chemicals") Wes pulled a few in and out of the water, brushing away the flies. He hung one to dry on the side of a shed.

Yes it stunk, and Wes thought it was funny that I noticed.

All of a sudden he had a long and sharp machete in his hand, seemingly out of nowhere. I could not help but flash back to the Psycho of Mendo.

"Hi Daddy hi," said Wes's daughter, no bigger than the machete. And she ran over and hugged him around the thighs. Wes has seven kids with four different wives. I didn't count but there were lots of little faces there.

"I divorced all of them because they got drunk. I can't be around that."

He showed me a stretching post, a piece of wood now smooth with 15 years of use. Two days later, I found out from watching the TV show Dirty Jobs that the skins are soaked for a while, then the stiff pelts are dragged over a post to make them supple. This piece of was now smooth as ivory.

He showed me a collection of moccasins, skirts, shirts, cradleboards and other items he made from items that were stinky and kind of gross just a few days before. I think he expected me to know a lot more about it than I did.

But time was a wastin' – we had some hunting to do before nightfall.

Elizabeth's son Docavi, came out to help us load the truck. "You're pretty big," I told him. "You play basketball?"

When he said yes, I showed him two moves on the court that always, always, work.

His mom was smiling. Though I wasn't sure why. When I asked Wes if it was going to be OK for him to show up with a hitchhiker in tow, he said "she didn't have anything to say about it."

Dacavi was happy and promised to use the moves on the court the next time he played. Wes pushed his gun into the front seat and we were on our way – 100 miles to the hunting ground.

"This is the first gun I ever had," he said, making it around 40 years old. It was a .22 caliber that looked more like a pipe with a piece of wood tied on. But Wes was a hunter, there was no doubt about that.

At WalMart, buying bullets, we talked hunting with the clerk. Wes told him about Rockchucks, aka groundhogs, and he told us about hunting squirrels. In these parts people do not talk about killing animals for recreation. But food. Or in some cases, survival.

Growing up, I saw squirrels every day of my life. It never occurred to me or anyone I knew from that part of the world to ever hunt or eat one. But according to the clerk, we had it all wrong.

"My friends are coming up from Texas this week and we're going squirrel hunting," he said. "Last time we got 367 of them. They're good. All you do is put one in a pressure cooker for 15 minutes, then take 'em out and fry 'em up. Taste like fried chicken. Real good."

Whatever.

Ninety miles down the back roads of Northern Nevada, we turned onto a dirt track. Wes stopped the Caddy and lit a stick of sage.

"I'm going to pray now," he said, getting out of the car and walking around it the way I used to do with incense at funerals when

I was an altar boy. Years later, I would buy Tommy Bahama cologne that smelled identical.

Then Wes went up a nearby hill, bowed to the four corners, did some more praying, and off we went.

"I left some bread and tobacco and money on the hill. The ancestors like gifts."

It seemed like the praying was at least as much to the ancestors as it was to the gods and the animals we were after. I had a vision of them huddled around praying that Wes's car broke down.

Wes broke the reverie with a warning. "Now this has to be a secret. Don't tell anybody we are out here hunting. This is supposed to be for Indians only."

Alright, so I'm not that bright.

That sounded fine by me.

So we set out looking for antelopes. And deer too, I think. All the while Wes was telling me about the animals, where they hang out, what they do at different times of the day, and how that would help us find them. All mixed in with the lore of the Pautes of Northern Nevada.

We were pretty close to the mountains, and to Wes, each peak was nothing more than some kind of road sign, each marking the way to another hunting ground or friend's house or relative's ranch.

"Looked like we spooked some horses," he said, pointing to a herd of about 25-30 horses some 200 yards away. I actually knew my distances better than Wes – it's a golf thing. I told him about my golf range finder that uses a laser and he seemed incredulous.

Anyway, the ponies kicked up a thick cloud of grey dust as they broke into a gallop.

I thought they were going to run away from us into the nearby hills and bushes. But they did not.

"Hey Wes, they're getting closer," I said. At this point this city kid was very impressed. Soon the horses were running parallel to us around 25 yards away. We could hear them snorting and breathing and of course their hooves beating.

Then they cut to the left and ran across the road right in front of us, as Wes brought the car to a crawl. Two other herds did the same thing over the next 30 minutes. At first I thought they were afraid and running from us. But now it seems they were playing with us like dolphin swimming in the wake of a fishing boat.

We saw hundreds of horses, but only one antelope that also cut right in front of us and bounded away for the hills before Wes could stop the car and get his gun.

"The horses are mean to the antelope," Wes said. "Sometimes they kick them." He would know. Definitely.

Soon it was dark, and we turned the Caddy home, another 100 miles. "I'm taking Docavi hunting tomorrow, you can come if you want. We're getting up at 4."

To and from, we did a lot of talking. Wes hated drugs and booze and just about everyone he grew up with was addicted to one or the other. Or both.

Wes tried to live his life full of Indian traditions. He believed that so many of this buddies were in trouble because they strayed from the hunting, fishing, praying and other rituals that gave meaning to the Paute. Or at least to Wes.

Soon it was midnight and I was on the couch, asleep in less than a minute. Four hours later, we were digging into plates of eggs, potatoes and some kind of game meat, which for some reason I did not have the nerve to try. But the coffee was great. Nice and strong.

For all the great things I say and think about the great people of the Midwest, this also has to be said: They drink lousy coffee. So I appreciated that. Nuff said.

We set out, this time with Docavi. He had yet to kill a deer or big animal and Wes was hoping today would be his first. It struck me as some kind of Confirmation ceremony, and I was happy to be along, remembering my own Confirmation when my brother Kevin in his uniform as my sponsor.

Oh yes I was proud.

"For the first hunt, we believe it should be a good one," said Wes. "The antlers have to be large enough for a boy to crawl through them when you turn the animal upside down."

50 miles later we stopped next to a hillside full of large rocks. Wes got out and whistled at sharp and short and loud pitch. Almost a yelp.

"Sometimes, at sunrise, they come out. The rockchucks. When you whistle, they come out to see what is going on."

Now remember, we were at a restaurant, not a zoo. And when something like a ground hog has a cute name, you know it is because someone likes eating them.

Had fuzzy wuzzies poked their heads out of the rocks, Wes would have had them on the table within 24 hours. And their skins on the shed soon after. After hearing Wes's call, I was kind of surprised when hundreds of them did not start some kind of stampede towards us.

In fact, I kidded Wes that we should not even have to drive to find the animals but that he should call them into his front yard where we could take care of business right there.

But there would be no rockchucks that day.

As we headed out for the hunting grounds, I talked to Docavi about school and sports. The usual. He said he was disappointed that school had just ended the day before because he had a B that he wanted to turn into an A.

He was serious.

Soon, Wes gently hinted that I was talking too much and that Docavi had to get his mind straight so that we could find some antelope.

So we piped down for five minutes before when Wes started jabbering about hunting and the U.S. government and how they screwed the Indians.

Over the nearly 24 hours I was with Wes, I figure I was scanning countryside for game about ten hours. Listening to the evils of the U.S. government was a close second.

To his credit, he seemed to sense that buying into the whole victim thing was not going to do him any good.

I mentioned to him the books of Tony Hillerman, novels set on the Navajo reservation. And how the big difference between Indians and white folks was the Indians could tolerate silence, whites could not. And how the Navajo detective used silence to extract confessions when the white suspect could not longer stand the silent treatment.

He laughed and got us back to business. "Keep looking. Six eyes are better than two." But we did not see any game. Lots of cows, but nothing else. I told him about a game warden who picked me up a few weeks back who had come across some rich hunters in the wild.

They had shot a mule and thought it was a deer.

We were heading back, resigned to the fact that we would return antelope-less, when two bucks sprang out of the brush and crossed in front of our car.

"They're going to stop right there," Wes said as he stopped the Caddy.

He could have said "cue the antelope" and it would have had the same effect: They stopped right where he said they would. 25 yards away. Just staring at us. Me.

I wanted to shoo them away as I heard Wes get out. "Give me some bullets, quick. Give me some bullets," he whispered to Docavi, on full alert in the back seat.

I mentally begged them to run, knowing that made me a bad guest and all that. I didn't care. Soon I heard pop and load. Pop and load.

He shanked it. He somehow missed at few antelope at a distance we could have brained them with big rocks. I breathed in relief as the antelope ran away. But they stopped again

All the while Wes was squeezing off shot after shot. Shoot, reload. Shoot.

"Come on Docavi, I think we got one." Then he turned to me. "Colin, Docavi and I are going to get the antelope. You take the car down the road. If anyone comes by, any Indians or anybody, don't tell them anything. Come back in 15 minutes. Don't say anything."

Fine by me. So that's what I did, taking the time to notice the wind was blowing hard – three clubs hard. No wonder he missed.

15 minutes later, I put the Caddy in gear to meet the great hunters as they returned to the road carrying their prize. As I approached, Wes and Docavi were hiding in the bushes, lying flat and frantically waving at me to keep going. I looked up and saw a car on the horizon heading our way.

Ten minutes later the car was gone and I was back helping them load the antelope into the trunk. Of the Cadillac. It could have been some kind of bank robbery or kidnapping, that's how much speed and urgency we used before making our get away.

We were definitely in a hurry.

With Wes driving, we headed down the road, drying blood covering his hands and spattered neck.

I must have known it all along but now I knew for sure without even asking: We were poachers. Taking antelope without regard for seasons or permits or lands or anything like that.

"There's still one out there, Docavi," said Wes. "Here, go see if you can find him." And with gun in hand, Docavi headed into the brush at a jog as Wes and I drove about 100 yards down the road to see if we could head him off.

Soon we were driving the Caddy through a deeply rutted and slightly muddy track. Wes pointed at some kind of salt flat in the distance. "Come on, let's go down there and we'll meet Docavi."

I was never impressed with any Cadillac as much as I was with that car that day. It went over hill and dale and bump and brush without a problem.

If ever a Cadillac covered rougher ground with fewer problems all the while carrying a dead antelope with its grey tongue hanging out in the trunk, I could not imagine it.

But there would be no more antelope that day. After two days of hunting, we saw three antelope.

"Wes, up in Wyoming, we saw about a thousand antelope near the road over about six hours," I said. "They are everywhere."

"And Indians are going hungry up there? That's crazy."

Wes thought that every poor Indian should be feeding his family from wild animals. But most did not know how. That's why it was Wes's dream to put on a demonstration of Native American wildlife skills at the Smithsonian.

Wes sold some of his goods via catalogue to people who lived in Northern Nevada. When he picked me up, he was on his way to drop off some moccasins to the lady who owned the general store.

"Ever thought about selling your stuff on E-Bay?" I asked, stating the obvious. "or Craigslist?"

He looked at me as if this were some kind breathtakingly new idea. I offered to help. But I was unsure if he sincerely did not know about Craigslist, or was just being polite to the city kid with a funny backpack who did not know anything about hunting or antelopes or rockchucks.

But who knew a little bit about basketball. And that was nothing at all. Soon we were getting close to town. The mood was lighter now that we had some meat and skin and bragging rights for the women.

I took a few pictures. "Alright, don't over do it," he said. And, after an admonition to call him right away if saw any dead eagles on the road, he was gone.

Yes, there is a big old antelope in the trunk of that car.

Chapter 43

Ed and Helen: A Love Story in Two Parts

Part I.

"Helen's mother spotted me at the gas station. I had just spent five years in the army and it my first day at work pumping gas. Eugene, Oregon. December 1963.

Helen's mom went home and told her about a new guy at the gas station who looked pretty good. Helen had a boyfriend but her parents did not like him. So they sent her down to gas up the car.

They had four of them.

That was back in the day when people signed their credit card receipts and handed over the hard copy. But Helen took off with the hard copy and I thought I was going to get stuck with the bill.

An hour later, she was back, all happy and laughing as she returned the hard copy.

She came in to get gas every day for three months before I figured out what was going on and asked her out. In March 1965 we got married.

Part II.

Eight years ago we moved from Eugene to Apache Junction, Arizona to take care of Helen's parents. They are both over 85. He's retired but she is still big in real estate, buying and selling homes in foreclosure. Fixing them up.

The other day, she asked me to go to WalMart to pick up some supplies for the people fixing one of her homes. I told her if I was going to work for her, I'd have to get paid.

She got mad at me.

Chapter 44

Colin's Complete Rules for Hitchhikers

Keep you zipper zipped at all times. While on the road.Avoid prisons and brothels.

That's about it.

They gave me a ride through town, then came back to return the headphones I had left in their car. Their kids are in the back seat, fresh from Little League.

Chapter 45

More Free Food In Nevada

Just a few minutes into my career as a big game poacher and a late model car with a fat guy wearing a hat pulls over.

The first car to pass me. Luck.

I bent over and looked at my benefactor.

"Need some food?" he asked.

"No, I'm good, thanks, though."

"How about a pack or a blanket or sleeping bag?"

Couldn't this guy tell I was a big time hunter now? Hell, I could hunt a few woodchucks and skin them if I thought I needed something to keep me warm.

"No, thanks."

I looked over and between the seats in the front were 10 or 20 single dollar bills scattered all over.

"How about summer sausage? You like summer sausage? Its good. How about some summer sausage?"

This was Pierre, South Dakota all over again. Free food.

The driver may have wanted to spread the wealth, but unbeknownst to the big guy making all the offers, the passenger was having none of it. He was sneering in his scuffy clothes and dirty hair.

This guy was clearly just a few minutes from the streets and he had already figured out that every piece of summer sausage that made its way into my belly came directly from his.

"Just wanted to make sure you were OK," said the driver. And he pulled away, clearly wondering about what kind of hitchhiker is fool enough to turn down some summer sausage.

For the first time the passenger smiled.

Chapter 46

Colin and the Telecom Nomads

These guys are everywhere.

"You are not a killer or robber are you?"

"No, I'm a writer. Blah, blah, blah. "

"Me too, I'm a playwright."

And he was too. So off we went, 200 miles south towards Vegas, in the company of a pack of telecom nomads.

Don, the guy who picked me up, was one of 10 guys in a crew who traveled the country installing and repairing cell phone towers.

"My boss passed you a few minutes ago and called to tell me to pick you up," he said. So we talked writing and writers and books and how he had written two plays.

An hour later the caravan was stopped for pizza and beer. "Come on, Steve the boss wants to meet you."

Pretty soon the whole gang of us were sitting around a few tables jabbering about Springsteen, football, East Coast sub sandwiches, and the last guy they picked up hitchhiking.

"He was dirty and smelly. Alcoholic," said Steve the boss. "We called him Shakey because until he had his first beer his hands shook. So I cleaned up him. Got him some clothes, a shower, the whole thing and gave him a job. He was a good worker but one day his birthday came around and he started drinking again and never really stopped. So I had to fire him."

"Did you know he had a degree in psychology and played minor league baseball?" Don said.

Everyone at the table shook their heads from side to side.

Dave, the other boss, sat across from me and talked about his days playing in a rock band at the Stone Pony – which to Springsteen fans was the equivalent of Highway 61 to Dylan fans.

Dave and Lisa, the boss's girlfriend, were not fans of their New Jersey hometown hero. "We used to call him Bruce 'can't sing' steen," said Dave as Lisa vigorously agreed. Ouch. Dissing the boss.

We parted in the late afternoon around 200 miles from Vegas. They checked into a hotel while I pressed on. Ten minutes later, I was on my south another 100 miles where I arrived with plenty of daylight.

With visions of Vegas dancing in my head, I stuck my thumb out. But there would be no rides that night. Tonight I would bed down in a small hotel in Death Valley, not too far from the brothel up the street.

No wonder so many truckers pass through this town.

The next morning I stood in front of the Death Valley Inn in the cloudy, 75 degree weather. For June that was lucky, might lucky.

Just as a Springsteen song came on my radio, a big pickup stopped and from inside I heard, "Hey Colin, get in."

It was Dave, the guitar playing boss.

"Hey Dave, guess who's on the radio? Springsteen?"

He smiled as I climbed up and in. "Did you go to the party last night?"

He was surprised when I said no. Somehow, after spending an afternoon with the Telecom Nomads, I was expected to go to all their parties. Which I gathered involved playing pool and talking to the local girls.

And we spent the next 100 miles gabbing about Rush Limbaugh and troublesome sons. Soon we approached Vegas and stopped for the best subs and cheesesteaks this side of the Mississippi.

He dropped me at Bally's on the strip, where I poured myself into a great suite for a 5 day stay complimentary, thank you very much. Where I tried to find time to smoke the two great cigars Dave gave me as we said goodbye.

Chapter 47

Robert Frost Goes to Vegas

Robert Frost said "home is the place that when you have to go there, they have to take you in."

Needing a place to call home for a few days, I naturally found myself at the Bally's casino in Las Vegas. When my business slowed down a year or so ago, so did my trips to Vegas.

But offers of free rooms at the nicest places in town kept coming via email right on schedule.

But first I would have to find a phone, my Iphone was still in Iowa. It took an hour and several incredulous looks from casino employees before someone could successfully direct me to a pay phone. Not having a cell phone is today's unforgivable social sin.

Finally I found a pay phone, hidden way in the back of a little used part of the casino.

A few minutes later I was giving some pleasant stranger a number on a player's card, and, as if I were rubbing a magic lamp, a wish for five free nights free at their hotel was granted.

I must have lost more money that I remember at these places. They were all too eager to have me.

But soon all the grime of a few days on the road was swirling away down a very nice bath tub in a large and comfortable suite, thank you very much.

It takes a while to figure this out, but Vegas probably has more normal people than any other city in the country.

Despite the movies and whatever, most people in Vegas are not bumping boogies with Paris Hilton at some crazy fancy nightclub.

Most are just normal, if not slightly upscale people who would like to find some trouble or excitement, but more to tell the folks back home than actually be a part of it.

This is the greatest city in the world. And every staid urban planner should be required to spend some time here to take in the whimsy and creativity and explosive imagination it took to make it happen.

Then they should be required to add some of that to every project they poo-poo so often before feeding it to a grinder that makes them all come out the same.

Anyway ...

The Most Important Thing You Will Ever Read about Jazz.

Across from the hotel, I found myself walking past a dirt lot that was crappy even by dirt lot standards. The sidewalk, however, remained. And it contained a walk of fame containing big brass plaques imbedded in the sidewalk surrounded by church-like Italian marble.

All commemorating famous jazz musicians such as Louie Armstrong, Ella Fitzgerald, Buddy Rich, Duke Ellington, and seven or eight others. A few yards down was space for another dozen plaques.

Whatever they were yesterday, today they welcomed people on the way to and from a bus stop in front of a dingy grocery store next to the dirt lot littered with bottles and boxes.

Someone learned about jazz the hard way. Just as my buddy Dan and I had.

Dan, also known as Base Camp, took a small soda shop and bait shack at the end of a pier and turned it into yuppie hangout, complete with palm trees, live music, and expensive coffee.

Thousands of people walked by the place every day, amazed at the turnaround, and dozens every day looked in, almost in wonder, and said "You guys should have jazz there."

We were not fans of jazz, but Dan said 'why not?" And for some reason San Diego had lots of famous jazz players who were eager to play, including many people who played with the same people remembered and forgotten in marble and brass in Vegas today.

So we kicked out the guitar playing kids and replaced them with a guitar and drums and piano and maybe a trumpet and sometimes someone to sing.

Aging hipsters walking by saw the jazz kit and told us how great it was we had jazz.

It was a disaster.

Jazz fans are cheap. I cannot tell you how many times someone would come in and ask for hot water then pull out a tea bag.

Not many people showed up. And we promoted it just fine, in case you were wondering.

As soon as Dan went back to finding some dirty looking young guys who somehow could keep a reggae beat on two old guitars and a beat up old drum, hundreds and hundreds of kids would arrive early, stay late, and pay ridiculous amounts of money for a can of Budweiser.

Now our money-losing experiment in jazz had its own monument on the sidewalks of Las Vegas.

But I had bigger things to worry about than decaying plaques to ancient and forgotten musical cults. I was breaking my oldest and firmest rule: Only go to Vegas with lots and lots of money.

And soon as my free rooms went away, I would have to find a way to refill the old pockets. I'll have to check and see what Robert Frost has to say about that.

If you want to visit the most realistic memorial to the true nature and appeal of jazz, I have just the street corner memorial for you in beautiful Las Vegas Nevada.

When I pulled into the town where I grew up a few days later, they were in the middle of a Jazz festival.

Chapter 48

Father of the Year. Not.

On my way out of Vegas, I took a city bus to Boulder City and contemplated my former status as Father of the Year, a badge I always wore with pride. Self-awarded as it may have been. But no more. Today I officially turn it in. In its place, I'd like to decline the Asshole of the Year Award, but apparently once nominated you cannot turn it down.

Though divorced, I always lived within a few blocks of my two kids. I saw them every weekend and often more. Never late. Never canceling. Not even once.

I did the coaching thing, the school thing, the take them to faraway places with their friends thing. I told my son about girls and how to talk to them. "Ask them if they want a Coke. Tell them they look nice or dance well or you like the way they answer questions in class. Anything. Just get something started."

During my own time as a seventh grader, George Callahan and I met some girls near Boy Scout Camp. He was talking up a storm, laughing, smiling, joking. The girls liked it.

When they left he turned to me. "Why didn't you say something," he asked. I didn't answer.

Using the classic path of teaching your own kids what you learned too late to do you any good, I set out to make sure that by the time my kids were 18, they would speak a foreign language, excel at a sport, and play a musical instrument.

Each got 2 out of 3. Which is good considering most second string shortstops have higher batting averages than most parents.

I taught my son how to fight. To protect himself and his sister.

The school had a rule that said both kids fighting would be kicked out. I told him if anyone picked on him or his sister, he better damn well take care of business right then and there and I did not care if he got kicked out or not.

So that is 3 our of 4, as far as he goes.

I still believe the single greatest piece of parenting advice that I or any other parent ever gave a kid was when I told my 11 year old son he should practice the guitar because "chicks like guys who play guitar."

I did not know it at the time – at least not consciously – but this counsel came just minutes after his hormones kicked in.

I never had to say another word about practicing or playing the guitar.

Once I picked up my son from grade school on a motorcycle. "My dad's taller than Michael Jordan," he said. Years later his friends told me that.

Girls are of course different, as all children are different from each other – only more so. Walking through the playground with my daughter, children would hang out of windows from 50 yards away to say goodbye to her.

Where did that come from?

My parent of the Year nomination for her came after The Talk. About Men, of course. I did it in the car so neither of us could escape. It wasn't gynecological. That's what moms are for.

This was to reveal the secrets of men. "Alright Goobler," which is what I called her though she stopped liking it a few months later but I never stopped calling her that. "Here is what it is like to be a man. Stop eating for 2/3 days. At the end of the second day, everything you see will remind you of food. The stop sign? An apple. A tree, a salad."

"Everything you smell will set your taste buds on fire. Someone barbecuing a mile away? The burnt steak molecules will seek you out and taunt you.

"Food, food, food. Everywhere.

"By the third day, you can feel the hunger in your throat, your fingers, your face, let alone your belly.

"That is what sex is like for a guy. Especially a teenage guy.

"We need it bad. But once we get it we don't need it anymore. So if you ever want a guy to stop liking you, just have sex with him too soon. That will do it. Guaranteed."

I looked over to see if she was taking any of this in. "You want to hear any more about this or you want me to stop?" I asked. "Go on. Go on. I'm listening."

And I think she was, too.

They both got out of high school, mostly unscathed. No jail. No drug addictions. No alcoholism.

For that alone, I kept my Father of the Year Award burnished bright. Always ready to bring it out and show it around if my friends' kids were in a jam.

That of course was breaking my own rule: Any time you congratulate yourself on your great parenting skills, THE PHONE CALL would follow, often in just minutes.

Pride goeth before the fall,. Or did it cometh?

Anyway, a week or so ago, I was poaching big game in Northern Nevada. I thought my buddy and ride and house host was a bit stern with his girlfriend's son. But the 8th grader seemed to respond well and enjoyed hunting with Wes.

Two days later, I listened to one of my rides tell me about how he raised his son with plenty of spankings and harshness. I heard my usual reaction, this time only in my own mind.

"Spanking is usually a sign that the parent is out of control, not the kid," I told my friends dozens of times over the years. But this son grew up straight and tall with great affection for his dad.

While mine writes me letters he is unhappy with me because he did not like the way I referred to him when I talked to my cat.

For the last two days, I've ridden to and from the library on a bus in Vegas. One day I sat in front of a mom who verbally assaulted her three year old girl for the entire trip. By the time I got off, the little girl was either ignoring her, or giving back as good as what she got.

That night, the local news had a story of a three year old girl found dead in a dumpster. I checked the picture to make sure it wasn't her. That's how bad it was.

Yesterday, a woman young and heavy and tattooed got on the bus with her two children and migrant farmer boyfriend who was clearly not the dad. For the next 45 minutes, they screamed and cried and yelled at high volume. That's all they did.

When the fat lady sat down, she reached across the aisle and slugged here 5 year old daughter in the should for no apparent reason. "Ouch, why'd you do that. That hurt," screamed the girl.

"You just don't get it," said the mom. "If you did, you wouldn't have to ask."

All the while the toddler cried and begged for his momma. After 15 minutes, she took him from the guy who was about 2/3 here size and smiled like some kind of wounded wolf.

With two free hands, he was now free to smack the girl in the face. They laughed while the girl cried. In between guffaws, he put his hand up to his nose, three stooges style, and told he she should have blocked it.

Then they laughed some more.

All I'm saying is that I may have Parent of the Year, but the competition was not that tough.

I not only allowed, I encouraged my kids to watch the Simpsons. That is when teachers and parents regarded this practice to something akin to fat ladies on buses beating their children.

After my nomination as Asshole of the Year, no century, I reached Base Camp on the wireless.

"Dan, my kids think I'm an asshole now. Did I ever do any of that bad stuff when they were younger?"

"Hell no," he said. "You were a good parent."

He knew them for a long time. Saw them often. They used to roam up and down the Ocean Beach Pier, making friend with other kids by telling them they could come to Dan's restaurant/bait shop and have as much candy as they wanted.

We laughed about that. Those kids were popular. So I told Dan the background for my latest nomination.

"A few months ago, I asked Caitlin to store a few things in her garage. She said she couldn't. Wouldn't. I was quite unhappy with that and told her the worst thing any family member could say to another was that they were counting on you and you let them down."

"So she sends me an email while I'm in Vegas saying I should come and visit. Prior to that email, I had no intentions of returning to California. Been there. Done that. But I thought I could hitchhike through Death Valley in the summer, see my family, get this manuscript in order, and get my clothes together. So I told her it would take me two weeks to do all that. She said I could stay two days, max. I was quite unhappy about that."

Dan and I commiserated and he wondered what had gotten into his two earth angels.

I didn't know. But I was sure I was not going to spend the next 20 years of my life with my kids behaving badly and me acting sadly, like some Dear Abby letter that I used to read but never believe because it was too preposterous.

Not anymore. Sorry about that Abby.

So instead of heading to San Diego and circling San Francisco like a vulture while I awaited my client to shower me with duties and ducats, I would head east to Delaware.

Damn. That's where I was headed but not really where I wanted to go. I kicked myself back into a good humor. Like Vegas, my only rule for traveling there was to make sure I was at the top of my game and my pockets were brimming with cash.

That wasn't happening. And not letting on would take a lot of work.

Chapter 49

Gall bladders over Vegas.

So now I'm on the road to the East Coast. In five hours I've done about fifty miles, and I sit near Hoover dam wondering where I am going to sleep tonite to conserve cash.

This is not going to spoil my trip or run me down" I tell Base Camp of my dwindling cash supply. "I'll just make that part of the adventure."

Though I know Base Camp will throw money at me if he even has the slightest hint that I need it, even if he needs it more than me.

Hitchhiking in any city is problematic. So to get from the library to the hotel, I walk three miles, passing the hospital where I spent New Years day two years ago.

Bad gall bladder. Though apparently the only people on this planet who did not know that severe and regular stomach pains over a period of time were the classic signs of a bad organ were the people at the Emergency Care Center. And me.

So off I went with the world's greatest girlfriend, sirens wailing, to the emergency room.

For two hours I moaned and writhed and suffered in silence as guys are supposed to do. Doctors and nurses scurried to and fro, and not seeing any blood or bones, they put me on their 'he'll live for another hour' list.

In Vegas, or probably any emergency room, it takes a while to convince them you are really hurting and not just some junkie looking for free drugs.

I knew I had to go Academy Award dramatics on their ass if I was ever going to get the pain to stop. So I began moaning and groaning every time I saw anyone in a wearing white. Twenty minutes later a doctor came and grunted a few questions at me and soon a nurse was emptying a syringe into my IV.

I swear the needle was still in the bag when the gates of pharmaceutical heaven opened and instantly took me to a happy place where there is no word for pain. I looked around from my new and lofty home and wondered why and how every doctor in the world was not a stone drug addict.

And how today, if you stick your thumb out in any random corner North of San Francisco, someone will come along and offer to cure what ails you, even if nothin' is ailin' you.

Chapter 50

Hypocrites vs. Idiots

Vegas and kids and big old damns on my mind.

Outside of Boulder City, I'm looking at Lake Mead, with plenty of time to think about how I was not a perfect parent.

I do admit on several occasions while my kids were a bit too loud in the car while on our way to a weekend of snowboarding, threatening them with a 27 minute version of the Allman Brother's Whipping Post. Or worse, Dylan Blood on the Tracks.

I occasionally carried out these threats. And whether in the spirit of anger or discipline, I made them listen for the entire and agonizing 27 minutes.

Like I said, I never said said I was a perfect parent.

Just a good one, the perfect being the enemy of the good and and all that.

Perfect parents are the worst parents. They are always playing catch up

It's always about their guilt, not their kids. And that is what gets them in trouble.

They are the parents – usually single moms it must be said – who invite high school children over for beers and pot because 'I blew a little weed in high school and I can't be a hypocrite so I'd rather have them do it here where I can keep an eye on them.'

Idiot yes. Hypocrite, no.

A good parent knows how essential hypocrisy is.

(See how easy I slip into my Parent of the Year Bullshit. Even on the side of the desert road in Nevada. So I must warn you: Don't listen. None of this works.)

We have to set standards for our children that we ourselves did not – do not – meet.

I'm standing across the street from Saint Judas, some kind of hospice for kids I think. I'm writing this on a spiral notebook and I do not even notice or care if cars whizz by.

A mile or so down the road, Lake Mead backs up behind Hoover Dam. The sun is going down on a pleasant Nevada afternoon.

Chapter 51

Rules.

I don't really have that many rules about hitchhiking. The ones I do seem more like superstitions.

For example, I like to give potential drivers a visual back story – a reason I am where I am so they will stop.

Example, I'm standing in front of a hospice for kids called St. Jude Ranch for Children. My back story: I want people driving by to think I was visiting or working at St. Jude.

If these kids need an example that miracles exist, I hope they visit the Hoover dam just a few miles away. That should do the trick.

I'm wearing a white Titleist golf cap and a Bobby Jones golf shirt. That should give some kind of story to golfers.

I'm also holding a pad of paper and a pen and writing this but I have no idea what that is saying. That's why prisons and brothels are bad: Bad back stories. Hotels and campgrounds are good. So is rain. Being in the middle of nowhere all by yourself is also surprisingly good, though I do not know why.

Chapter 52

Click, click. Hiss, hiss.

Somewhere in Arizona, I think.

Ah, click, click, hiss, hiss. The sounds of air brakes bringing 80,000 pounds of heavy machinery, tires and cargo to a rolling, lurching, stop.

I had just spent a cold and sleepless night pacing back and forth on a small road about two hours into Arizona. I gave up my last chance at a hotel for a chance at one more ride – a couple of twenty-somethings who invited me into the bed of their pickup, where I huddled down looking at the desert stars while the cold wind sought me out just a few inches above.

Twenty minutes later they dropped me at 2 a.m. in the parking lot of 7-11, and after five minutes of what I was doing and where I was going, we finished off with some pictures and well wishes.

Rides were not happening. And neither was the radio. Sometimes a car would pass, and ten minutes later I would discover my hand still in the air, thumbing through the carless night.

I hunkered down under a tree near a bush and tried to close my eyes, without success. I remembered – not for the last time -- the Guy from Ukiah, who told me that even a thin blanket was better than nothing for getting to sleep. Swaddling and all that.

The cold and eternal night ended. I waved goodbye to the girl from the 7-11 who worked the night shift while her husband drove a hundred miles one way to work every day. Her 13 year old son was starting summer school for math and English. He wanted to stay home and work on cars.

Some day some one will explain to me why so many parents think throwing their kids in with boring teachers to read boring books – while stopping the kids from learning useful things about which they are truly passionate -- constitutes something called an education.

There are a lot of smart kids out there with parents who spend an entire lifetime trying to convince them otherwise, all because the parents cannot – will not -- figure out what their child wants to learn about.

When the Amish looking buy rolled by a few minutes after sunset and offered to take me down the road, I would have gotten in had he been going for hours in the opposite direction and had guns and drugs and violent felons in the back seat.

A great three days.

By 7 a.m., I was fed and warm, but tired. So stretched out under a bush some 50 yards from the road.

Soon I was out. Sooner still I was up. Ants. Bite. Bite. Bite. I think a few got me in the crotch, I'm not sure. But I was up and groggy, my back and side covered with grass and burrs. A truck approached as I stuffed a shirt into my bag.

With every ounce of intellect and instinct telling not to waste my time, I stuck out my thumb anyway, hunched over as I zipped up my pack.

Hiss, hiss. Click, click.

Thus began my 1800 mile trip with the King of All Truck Drivers.

I'm settling into the springy front seat of an 18-wheeled, 13'6 feet high, 53 feet long and ten-foot wide tractor trailer with all the bells and whistles.

And we're off.

"Where you headed?"

"Philly."

Got 'em again.

"I'm not going that far but I'll get you part of the way." Usually that meant 25 miles down the road. I didn't ask where he was going. He didn't tell. Nor did I tell him I just woke up from a 20 minute nap after pacing on the road all night in the 40 something degree Arizona night. But I think he knew.

We spent the next three days talking about family, friends, jobs, you name it. Where guys are concerned, do I even have to say we talked about chicks?

Bill, I realize almost right away, is the King of All Truckers: Equal parts John Wayne, Dr. Phil, Joe the Plumber, and The Buddah. After 30 years of driving, the 60-something King of All Truckers is tired of driving, but energized by talking about anything but that.

Two of his sons are in the ROTC, one Air Force, one Marine Corps. The King of All Truckers was in the 82nd Airborne, 'jumping out of airplanes" but did not make a career of it. "I did not like taking bullshit from anyone. Still don't."

I tell him about my travels, my book, and my experiences with the last men to see my brother alive before he died in Viet Nam.

"Ever been to the Wall?" he wants to know.

"No," I said. And I tell him that though I seem to talking freely about it now, I usually don't. I don't go to my brother's grave. The Wall. Veterans' Groups. Memorial Day ceremonies. Or anything like that.

Just talking about it with the King of All Truckers brings a familiar tug on my throat and a tingling behind my eyeballs.

"I've been there, though none of my friends are on it. You should go."

"Maybe," I said staring straight ahead at the hazy Flagstaff afternoon.

"I know a lot of people who didn't want to go, but once they did, they were glad," he said.

I wasn't moving.

"You know what your problem is, don't you." he asked. The cabin was getting kind of small only because the outside was beginning to disappear, collapsing on itself into my head.

That was a statement, not a question.

"Not really." Though I knew the answer better than I knew my own name.

"You haven't let go."

He stopped for a bit. Wondering if I was worth it. He started up again. "But it's time for you to move on. That's the way of the universe. Letting go. Your brother has. So should you."

I locked my eyes on pine trees perched on granite that suddenly reappeared outside the cab. They whizzed by, if anything in slow motion can whiz.

I was grateful for my cheap and dark aviator glasses.

"I don't want to let go."

Assistant Trucker.

Chapter 53

The King of All Truckers warm up.

The King of All Truckers was just warming up. I told him about another trucker – off duty in a pickup – who picked me up in Boulder City the evening before. How he and his wife and his two adult children live close together and visit each other often.

Everyone happy with each other.

"That's what I imagined my life would be like when I grew up," I said. "But now they think I'm an asshole and I'm tired of that."

As we passed into New Mexico, the King of All Truckers told me about his life as the youngest of five children. His mom divorced when he was five, and a succession of men followed – along with almost predictable amounts of alcohol and abuse.

"When I turned 15 I stood up and said no more," he said.

I didn't know if it was too late for the King of All Truckers. As it was too late for most people who told me this story.

Adult children of alcoholics. Not many get out alive.

The King of All Truckers did. Wounded, but very much alive. Whether it was the price he paid or the grace he received, the King of All Truckers now believes it is his mission on earth to tell the truth, usually unvarnished.

All the time. Right away. Probably the only person I know for whom this actually works.

The King of All Truckers had it all figured out for me too. The kid thing that is.

"Did you tell them why you were upset? Did you talk about it with them?"

"Not really," I said. "I'm one of those people who think that what people do is their way of talking. That's what I listen to. I usually ignore whatever words they are using to obscure the true meaning of their actions. – what they are really saying."

The King of All Truckers was not buying that. "Talk to them. Communicate."

I shrug and wonder if there is not enough communication – or if there is plenty of it and I just don't like what I am hearing.

I tell him how surprised I am that my life has turned into a letter to Dear Abby. And wonder how otherwise smart and good people get themselves into such a bad and stupid mess.

"I'm supposed to be some kind of hot shot media and communications guru. So it's kind of funny to find myself getting good communications advice from a trucker as we pass into New Mexico. We teach what we have to learn, I guess."

The King of All Truckers laughed then smiled all the way to Albuquerque.

Soon he pulled into a truck stop. His ten hours of driving over, he would park and spend the night. I thanked him, took his picture, and made him promise to check out my blog on myspace.

And that was it, so I thought.

That evening there would be no ride from this truck stop in New Mexico. And take it as a sign of grogginess that the next morning, after a few hours sleep on the side of the road, I was surprised when he pulled up again.

And again the next day outside of Missouri. And finally we were just a few hours from his destination, Columbus Ohio.

It was my turn.

"So what are you going to do when you retire."

Grunt. Grumble. Nothing.

"You ought to do something you love. You love Harleys. Lots of rich people have Harleys and need help with them. You could do that. Make lots of money too."

For the next half and hour we went back and forth, with mostly him talking about how he's seen talent and hard work all too often go unrewarded. I suggested that he had lots of talent and brains and could do something interesting and make a lot of money.

"Do you think I'm the kind of person who is interested in a lot of money?"

"That's a copout," I said. "You could do it if you would just get rid of these crazy attitudes towards rich people and success. Its good, you know. And lots of rich people are good too. That's why they are rich: They know how to get along with people."

I saw a glimmer. And we parted.

Chapter 54
Nuclear Hitchhiking

Twenty five minutes after Jake and his girlfriend Leslie learned they were pregnant with their third child, they were pulling over in a difficult spot to get me down the road. I was grateful. They were gracious and curious.

Soon I was accepting their invitation to stay at their house for the night, eating hamburgers at midnite. She asked to see my blog, and soon was reading about my escape from the psycho of Mendecino.

"Hey look Jake," she said, pointing at the computer. "Those two kids who gave him a ride just sent him an email. They're hitting him up already."

When Jake was out of the room, she told me how much she liked my writing and touched my forearm, soft and sweet and gentle.

Oh jeez, here we go.

Late as it was, tired as we all were, we had one thing to do before calling it a night. Jake had to put up a kennel for his full grown English mastiff.

It was already assembled, we just took it out of his truck, spread it apart, and put this huge dog in it.

"He likes to hunt," Jake said. "He goes into the woods and kills deer. Sometimes he brings back pieces of their legs or hoofs. It's kind of gross."

I'm not a big mastiff expert or anything like that, but even I knew that big dogs are bred to kill big things. And this was a bear killer.

Soon I was taking off my boots and stretching out on the couch. Jake slept in a chair, with his girlfriend a few feet away on a mattress.

Her sister and his boyfriend, along with their two year old baby, lurked nearby. They did not need to know that I was running on 2/3 hours of sleep from the last three nights.

Eight hours later I was saying goodbye to Jake as he went off to work and scarfing down some eggs and toast when Leslie's sister emerged from the back bedroom.

She and Jake owed her $20. From what I heard in the next 30 minutes, it could have been $20 million.

"Where's my fucking money?" she screamed.

Leslie herded her into the back room away from the groggy egg eater. Me.

Silence.

"I don't care. I don't know him," she screamed again.

Silence. Then in full throat.

"You had three abortions because you cheated. You're a cheater. You bitch."

Silence, again, from Leslie.

I don't care. I don't know him. I don't know him."

Him being little old me, of course.

Silence.

Then, "you fucked sean, you whore."

Silence.

"I don't care. I don't know him."

Silence. Then crash. The Sister from Hell was throwing her parents best glassware and dishes. Crash. Crash. Crash.

Soon Leslie was back in the front room, making sure my eggs and toast were satisfactory. For the first time, I watched an episode of CSI on TV. Dang. Lots of autopsies on that show.

Leslie smiled wanly and shook her head, apologizing gently and softly.

I waved it off and began to put my boots on. The worst boots in the world.

Leslie returned to the back room, where they repeated, word for word, silence for silence, insult for insult, everything they had just finished.

Soon Leslie was back in the front room with me, talking to Jake. Only this time she was the one yelling and Jake, from what I could tell, was asking her to tone it down in front of their house guest.

Only he was yelling at her.

Oh man.

A few minutes later we were in their truck, on the way to Jake's job site. They continued yelling at each other on the phone just about the worst things a couple can say to each other, while she apologized during the 30 seconds or so when their phone went dead and they were between cell phone towers.

"My life is hell," she said to me.

I looked at her, saying as suburban Columbus rolled on by. "it doesn't have to be that way," I almost whispered. Soon she was back on the phone, cursing Jake. Repeating the exact same conversation she had with him five minutes before.

"Why is my sister following me?" she yelled into the phone.

Silence.

"Why is my sister following me?"

Silence. Repeat. Silence.

Soon Jake was in the car. "How'd you sleep last night?"

"Fine. Thanks man," as if nothing had happened. And as far as I was concerned, nothing had happened. I was a guest. A grateful guest who silently wished his new found friends would stop creating for themselves their own private hell.

The car stopped and it was time for me to go. Jake shook my hand and I reached to the back and took her hand too while I thanked them.

"Don't forget to stay in touch," he said.

"Sounds good."

Chapter 55

Welcome To Crack Town

Please keep your boots on.

I didn't think I'd ever get out of Columbus. Finally at dusk, I'm at a road near some factories and railroad tracks. At the local convenience store, a black guy in a new white Escalade parks his car, opens the door, lets in another guy with a new white Corvette, and they drive away.

Ten minutes later they return. The guy gets back in his Vette, and for a minute before leaving, he stares at me eating ice cream with my boots off.

The Escalade driver waits. I leave carrying my boots. Somehow I know that I should hitchhike in my socks. Soon I'm climbing into a panel truck and the driver is telling me why he picked me up.

"You're in the middle of crack town. One of the most dangerous areas around. I thought I'd get you out of there."

And I was in my socks.

Chapter 56

The Last Day?

My six day mileage report since leaving Bally's in Las Vegas: 30, 200, 570, 600, 580, 45.

The last day. A day of extremes. A day that recapped the entire two months in 24 hours.

It started outside of Columbus in a quiet truck stop. Quiet is not good. A steady rain gave me half a chance to get a ride from this dark and lonely outpost.

With nothing happening, I settled in for a long evening's journey to the dawn when an 18 wheeler pulled up next to me.

I hopped up on the step and looked through the window at a trucker in his 20's with a nice smile and happy demeanor.

"Hey, thanks for stopping. East. I'm going East."

"Sorry, I'm going to Indianapolis," he said in a Russian accent. A thousand miles the other way. Dang.

It was dark. 3 a.m. dark. The rain was coming in light and heavy. Light and heavy. But with a hat and a jacket it didn't seem to make much difference. I could only tell the difference by looking at the nearby puddle.

I wasn't cold. Not yet. That would come later.. My back ached. My legs hurt and that guy and girl making out under the canopy while gassing up their car only made the night darker and desolation more remote.

I wasn't tired. If somewhere to sleep is not an option, than neither is getting tired.

I was looking at the ground, loosening up my back when, without hearing their car, I heard a voice over my shoulder. "Hey, where are you going?"

It was the two make out artists.

"Philadelphia." It was still far enough away to get a chuckle.

"We'll get you as far as …." Now here you can fill in the blank because people always name a tiny city on an obscure road that has absolutely no meaning to me.

But I always say the same thing: "Sounds good."

So off we went to Wheeling, West Virginia.

They were nice and friendly and open and eager to talk. "Do you mind if we smoke?"

"No, go ahead," By this time I had figured out they were probably not talking about tobacco.

So while they passed a pipe back and forth, we talked about Mendo County.

"Everyone up there smokes it, grows it, smells like it and talks about it all the time," I said. "And its legal," I said, glossing over the fine print as to whether it was legal or not. I'm not a drug lawyer, after all. I continued.

"Here's how they do it. In California, pot is supposed to be legal for medicinal uses." I did not bore them by stating the obvious this was a dodge that every pot smoker saw through no matter what kind of drugs they were taking.

"So you go the doctor and tell him anything you want. You have anxiety, depression, whatever. Just keeping talking till you say the magic words. Pretty soon you'll have a prescription – recommendation they call it – for marijuana. The first thing you do is laminate that piece of paper and put it somewhere safe. Some keep it in the glove box. Its your get out of jail free card."

"Sometimes the doctor will write how much you are supposed to take. This is how much you are allowed to grow. 25 plants seems to be about right. So you round up all your friends, get them to the doctor, get their 'recommendations,' on file and voila: You now have permission to grow hundreds of plants in a coop. Each worth $5000."

I gave them a few seconds to do that math while I remembered my pot education course back in Mendo. Those chocolate chip cookie eaters would be proud of me for remembering everything they said.

Of coursed, I was the only one not stoned out of my gourd, so the short term memory thing was no problem.

Jim had his own California pot experience. The clouds opened outside, taxing the ability of his wipers to keep up. Even so, he spent the about half of the next five minutes looking over his shoulder as he told me his story.

"I got busted for carrying a few pounds in California and it wasn't even my pot. But it was in my car and nobody wanted to say whose it was. So I did seven days for a crime I did not commit."

We were crossing lanes, hitting the shoulder while he finished his tale. The girlfriend kept the car on the road without fanfare.

Just then his cute 19 year old girlfriend passed 3-week old puppy over the back seat. They should have waited, she said, but it was in a bad home.

Jim was a singer and songwriter as well. And soon he was singing his original version of his time in the slammer. I just remember the song had the words "wrongfully convicted."

I kind of wanted a clever refrain, but even without one, I felt honored that he would sing it for me. "He's so smart," said the Make Out Queen. "I've never had a boyfriend who knows so much about so many things."

The Make Out King nodded. A guy with a guitar gets the cute chick again. You know it's good if it works for felons.

With good feelings and lots of promises to meet on MySpace, we parted ways in a Wheeling truck stop. "Don't forget the titty bars, they are down that way. Six of them," he said. A girl has to like a guy an awful lot to pretend not to notice when your boyfriend is giving directions to the best titty bars in town.

And she did. Not notice and like him, that is.

I thanked him for the tip, and started heading the other way. 50 yards down the road, Jim drove up and rolled his window down. "Hey man, you want some pot for the road?"

"No thanks man, I'm good." I think that is what the kids say when they are refusing generous offers of illegal substances. I gave him a fist pump and headed for the restaurant.

I grabbed a coffee and a Tastycake, and decided to greet the dawn on the black and wet West Virginia road just a few hundred yards away.

I arrived at the ramp an hour before sunup. Just in time for a wicked rain.

I lit up a cigar. My first in months. I bought them back in Columbus after Ozzie and Harriet dropped me off near a smoke shop. For some reason I thought I needed a cigar to restore harmony. It's an Indian thing.

And now was a perfect time. I lit the cigar, turned on my little radio to find Tom Petty playing one of my favorite songs, "Wont Back Down." I absorbed the ecstacy of a great smoke, a great song, in a great place at a great time. And that included the rain.

It was glorious.

I danced a bit. First to Petty. Then to a succession of Motown classics, then – and this was when I knew something magical was happening – the theme from Rocky III came on: Eye of the Tiger.

It felt great to be alive and sleep deprived.

Eventually the sun strolled into Wheeling and magic disappeared with the dark. Because it was raining I knew I'd get a ride just as soon as someone could see me. A few minutes later, a late model Cadillac turned the corner and headed right for me. It veered away, then stopped.

"Hey we're going to ..." You know the drill.

"Sounds good."

They were on their way to work in Pennsylvania and still working on the first few sips of their giant mugs of coffee, they were feeling good and happy and so was I.

"It's easier to get rides in the rain," I confessed almost as soon as I got in the car.

"Yeah, kind of like a sympathy fuck," said the Anthony, the driver.

"Yeah," and for a moment I tried to remember if any comely lass had ever sacrificed her virtue to me because she thought I needed some cheering up. Right away I decided it was either none of them. Or all.

Dang.

Still going on the blast of energy from their good times and nice car, soon my thumb was back out about 30 miles out of Wheeling, 6:30 or so.

My luck was running just fine: It was raining. Not enough to get soaked, but enough to get myself a sympathy ride.

Paul pulled up almost right away. Nice car. Nice guy. A drug counselor and former petty criminal.

"Junkies are smart," he told me. "You have to be to survive while doing all that dope. When I was an addict, I used to go to dumpster diving and find credit card receipts. I used the account numbers to send electronic money orders to my friends for $500. They kept $100 and gave me the rest. I did that for six months before using a shredder. I had a dozen scams like that."

I told him about Mendo and all the dope growing and dope culture up there.

"I don't know if pot is a gateway drug or not," he said. "But the people around it are bad people who will get you hooked on drugs. Which is reason enough to stay away."

We pulled up to a Starbucks and he bought me a drink. I looked over. He had been off drugs for ten years, he said. And he seemed like a guy who had his shit together. Nice clothes. Good color. Calm and smart and wise demeanor.

By the time I finished my coffee, we were outside Pittsburgh and it was time to blast me down the road.

I was feeling cocky: Great rides. Great weather. Getting close to my destination. And by now, since I was getting so close to Delaware, it was more about the destination than the journey.

I hit the convenience store for some breakfast and noted the hard rain but did not worry about it. Rain was my friend, after all.

Boldy I hit the road near the ramp. In a few minutes, my boots, already disintegrating around my feet, we soaked and heavy. My jeans were dark and sticky cold.

For the first time in the trip I was miserable and wet and nobody wanted to pick up the stray puppy dog headed for Delaware a few hundred miles away.

Something was wrong. I wasn't getting a ride when I should have been.

Two hours later a housewife and her 8-year old daughter poured me into the back of their mini-van. "I can't stand to see you out there in the rain," she said. "My husband's going top kill me for picking up a hitchhiker."

Within a few minutes I met my real nemesis. The Pennsylvania Turnpike.

I wouldn't figure it out for a few more hours, but this was the problem: Every entrance – East and West – to the turnpike, had just one ramp. After you entered, then you chose which direction you were going.

So when people passed, they had no way of knowing which one you wanted. So they kept driving.

She dropped me off in this crazy busy place that was more like a plaza, and soon enough a state trooper pulled up. Only this time there was no hail fellow well met crap. He just got on the loudspeaker and told me I had to move "down that road to the ramp."

I have to confess I did feel entitled to a free ride in the nice man's car. Yes, I was starting to feel entitled, big time. After all my experiences with cops over the last 7 weeks, I wanted this guy to give me a ride, buy me breakfast, dry my clothes, and get me to a safe and clean spot to sleep, then hitchhike. All while telling me his stories.

Not to be.

The ramp was a one mile stretch of freeway leading to another ramp that was less crowded and more remote. Which was just fine with me since I needed some sleep.

So after looking for a cheese steak without success, I found a McDonald's then headed back to my ramp. Taking out my copy of the Sunday New York Times, I spread it under a nice tree, damp ground and threatening sky and caught 30 minutes of antless, dreamless sleep.

Then back in business. But for two hours nothing. Because this was outside Pittsburgh, I resolved to ask Dennis Miller what there was about his hometown that was so unfriendly to hitchhikers.

I figured it was some kind of working class 'you shouldn't be out there looking for something for nothing' kind of thing – which was just fine by me because that was my thing too.

Nevertheless, I had to get a ride. Or live the rest of my life on a Pittsburgh on-ramp.

ONE MORE PSYCHO FOR THE ROAD.

Philip rescued me from that fate when he rolled up in a new Nissan sports car. Inside, the car had all the gadgets: A satellite radio. Car phone controlled from the steering wheel. GPS. And he looked put together as well. Nice hair cut, with blonde streaks and tips obviously put in by a stylist. New and well pressed clothes. Neat and classy shoes.

If it sounds as if I'm some kind of doorman at a swanky Manhattan night club, so be it.

It's not that I'm trying to see if people are good or bad. I'm just trying to figure out what they are all about by what they are presenting to me and everyone else on this planet.

The one thing I didn't get right away was this guy was stoned out of his gourd on crack. Which he was.

"I'm headed east," I told him.

He smiled back and said get in.

In a few minutes we were on the turnpike heading west. "I'm going to Kohl's to get some Columbia socks. They are on sale."

"I was going East, but that's OK, I'll just hop out later on."

His girl friend who was not his girl friend called.

"I just picked up a hitchhiker and we're going to get some socks," he told her over the car speaker phone.

The girl hesitated. At this point I thought it was just some middle class hangup about picking up strangers. Nope.

"Did you get ... the ... stuff ... yet ...?" She wasn't stammering. She was trying to use some kind of code to see when they were going to get together to smoke crack.

He told he'd call her back and then came the story: Dui, a point 23. His fourth one. But he kept getting out of jail time because he lived with his 78-year old mom and he had to take care of her. I was sure it was the other way around.

"I flashed back to a few lifetimes ago when I was riding in the back seat of the cop car in Minnesota, on my way North 100 miles. And how the cop and I talked about drug users and dealers who drive around with expired plates, drinking beer, smoking whatever, with one light out, who get stopped holding a few pounds of meth.

That was this guy. And he told me about it.

"Last week we were driving around smoking meth and this cop pulled us over. We threw the stuff out the window except for the pipe. My girl, my old girlfriend, stuck the pipe up her pussy and they never found anything."

Two months before he had flunked a random drug test while visiting his probation officer. That cost him 12 days.

Ten minutes after the first call, the girlfriend calls back.

"Did you really pick up a hitchhiker?"

And they have another crack conversation about socks and stuff and when are they getting together.

"She's going to come over my mom's house tonight. We'll smoke some crack and I'll get a blowjob out of it. Only I better have sex with her before we start smoking because that stuff makes my pecker go .."

And he held up his index finger and crooked it downward.

"They have chemicals for that too," I offered.

Great: I was now offering crack addicts advice on how to get more drugs.

We talked hitchhiking, and how I was surprised I was having trouble getting rides in the rain. I would not have to wait for Dennis Miller to set me straight on that one: "Nobody wants to get the inside of their car wet."

Out of the mouths of crack fiends.

By this time I had figured out the story: He worked for a beer distributor and lived with his mom. He kept getting fired and arrested and she kept bailing him out and giving him money.

Soon we were in and out of Kohl's, with some nice Columbia socks. He was acting and talking like the Mendo psycho, which I now know to be what crack smokers are like.

Like Mendo psycho, he was due for some jail time in a few weeks, and he wanted to get his crack affairs in order before then.

We were back on the road and he barely had any idea where he was, let alone where I wanted to go. So I just asked him to take me to the next exit east of where he picked me up, and soon he was dropping me off.

I wondered if there was anyone in the whole dang country who was not doing drugs, or planning on doing drugs in the next 45 minutes.

"Want some socks?"

Oh hell yeah. My socks and boots were soaked. Fresh socks would soon put me in a fresh state of mind.

"How about hat?"

I'd been wondering about that. "Did you notice my hat was dirty?"

"I didn't want to say nothing, but yeah."

Whew. My slightly beat up, Rogaine yellow hat did not come up to the standards of the Pittsburgh crack smokers. I knew that was bad so I finally took it off. I had thought it was some kind of talisman. Turns out it was just a dirty hat.

It was a black hat with a Rock Star energy drink logo on it. Fine.

"How about some gloves?"

Sure.

And off he went to meet his crack girl friend, leaving me at a wide and comfortable entrance to the PA turnpike.

By now I had figured it out. My nemesis, that is. And desperate times called for desperate measures. So using my notebook, I cranked up a sign with one letter: E.

For another two hours, nothing. And the radio pickings were slim as well.

So I checked my messages then called my brother Denny, my East Coast base camp, to tell him I was on my way and would probably be there late that night.

Now since my Iphone was in Iowa, I was using a payphone near the toll booth. And making two calls with change is time consuming and complicated by my lack of sleep that was making me forget phone numbers.

Finally I figured it out and was just finishing my second call when someone I now believe is the biggest brainiac I ever met taps me on the shoulder and says he going East and will take me for a "few bucks."

"Sure. What if I pay the tolls." He looked surprised as if this was some kind of overly generous offer. Not knowing if I was in for a few dollars or a few hundred, I opened his front door.

He was 60'ish with shaggy hair and stringy beard with a pickup truck that could have come from Mendo central casting for pot growers. It took him a few minutes or so to clear off his front seat. I still did not have any idea how he knew I was hitchhiking unless it was my backpack near the phone.

I didn't ask. He was going a hundred miles or so down the pike and I was all in.

Jeff, a Kesey Guy and that was just alright with me.

For the next two hours, I heard Jeff talk about his personal experiences with some of the greatest American writers of the 20th Century.

The guy was Ken Kesey's wrestling partner at the University of Oregon, for crying out loud. 177 pounds.

"He was a good wrestler. Conference champ. He didn't say much whenever we had a party at the coach's house. He just listened and watched everyone. We were in class one day and I asked him about a girl sitting a few rows ahead of us.

"That's Cathy. She's nice and smart and fun. But she doesn't put out. So I went over and talked to her and we didn't stop talking for 8 hours. She became my first wife."

We talked about the movie adaptation of One Flew Over the Cuckoos Nest. "I was on the set and told Jack Nicholson that he fucked it up. He just laughed and said "Yeah, but we bought it."

Jeff had spent some time in Aspen when Hunter Thompson had just moved there. He reminded me of the story of Claudine Colbert, wife of singer Andy Williams. Colbert shot her ski champ boyfriend Spider Savitch and basically got off with seven days in jail.

Hunter Thompson.

"At the same time Thompson was found guilty of pissing in the alley of the Hotel Jerome in Aspen after a night of drinking. So they put him in jail for 30 days. He used to like to point out that killing someone in Aspen gets you a week in jail, but pissing in an alley gets you a month."

"Thompson liked guns and was always killing things," Jeff said.

I reminded Jeff of a column Thompson wrote for the San Francisco Examiner where he talked about shooting a fox then maiming it somehow as a message to other foxes.

"Hunter Thompson committed suicide 40 years ago but no one figured it out till last year," I chimed in, telling about a column on Thompson I had written for Aspen.com. "He was dead the moment he realized that instead of being a writer he was going to be a clown with a fistful of pills and bottle of whatever he used to amuse his rich and famous and usually younger friends."

Jeff had been to Hunter's home and drank with him at Woody's tavern outside Aspen. "Hunter was always killing things. Bears, foxes, whatever. In or out of season. Whenever they came to arrest him for it, he said the bear was charging his wife and that is why he had to shoot it."

And on and on we went. Talking books and everything else that Ginsburg, Ferlinghetti and Neal Casady wrote and did. And that was a lot. And he was there.

"Are you a college professor?"

No. Petroleum engineer."

Before I had time to figure all this out, we had run out of turnpike.

He gave me his card and promised to read a draft of this manuscript.

I was so absorbed in what we were talking about, I had not been paying attention to where we were going. I somehow thought we were somewhere near Harrisburg, close to the more than 100 first and second cousins I had in the area.

I was late afternoon and I had plenty of time to get there from here.

So when I saw the "Welcome to Maryland" sign, I was just as shocked as if it had said "Officer Julie Welcomes You to Canada."

I grew up not 60 miles from that town, but I never heard of it, let alone visited it. But it was some kind of major road crossing with lots of signs pointing the way to Baltimore and Washington and Harrisburg and just about everywhere else on the globe.

But it was raining. Days without proper sleep were catching up to me. My cash was disappearing. I was sick of the road. Sick of this book. Sick of adventure. Sick of hitchhiking. But I still had another 80 miles to go. I wanted to go home to Wilmington, Delaware.

For that, I would need the Heroes of Hockessin.

Whatever the name of the crazy little Maryland border town with lots of stores and trucks and tourists, I just wanted to get out of there. But I first I had to solve a turnpike problem: The only ramp out of town led to about a zillion destinations in a zillion different directions.

I needed another sign.

So broke out my notebook and pen and started fashioning the two letters that I hoped would get me home: DE.

Yes, I had lost my faith.

The day before my horoscope warned me that I was "quite caught up in the task at hand its turning out to be rather frustrating. Its possible that you are forgetting why you wanted to do it in the first place."

Desperation breeds superstition. True.

But I also realized how easy it is to feel untethered. Once your family goes off, once your job slows down, once your friends have their own lives to take care of, the ties that bind can lift you like a weather balloon. Picking you up and setting you down almost at random.

I needed to get tethered again. Back to my people, however remote they were.

And that is what I was supposed to be doing with my little sign when I heard a horn honk behind me.

The Heroes of Hagerstown

A truck. I wasn't sure it was for me. That happens sometimes. Trucks stop for a million reasons. But this was for me.

Chad was going to Hagerstown. Which was somewhere between where I was and Baltimore. At that point I was in Jimmy Buffet's "Somewhere Other Than Here Mode. "Great. Let's go."

I climbed up and settled into Chad's world of tools and lifts and pumps and radios and everything that a guy who builds cell towers needs to live on the road.

"My buddy just passed you. I'm surprised he didn't pick you up." Then Chad called his friend Barry, who was getting ready to turn around and do just that.

He offered me a Gatorade and we started talking about Heavy Metal groups and how he met his girlfriend in Daytona when he took his Harley down there for a rally. Chad had lots of tattoos, and his beefy fit torso spoke of a time playing high school football.

"Yeah, we pick up lots of hitchhikers," he said. "Just a few days ago, at that spot, we pulled over for an old black guy, must have been 70 years old. We pulled over and asked if he wanted a ride. It was in the middle of the day and hot. He said 'what you boys want to give me a ride for. You going to mug me or something?' Then we asked if he wanted something to drink. Gatorade. He said he didn't "drink that crap.'

Chad was laughing. He continued. "We said 'we're just offering you a ride man. You were hitchhiking. No big deal to us. He said 'I suppose you boys are going to make me get in the back?' No. you sit up here with us."

Finally, Chad and Barry left him there, right where they picked me up. They still can't figure it out. I suggested that, though you never hear about it, some black people just don't like white people. For whatever reason.

We talked about Sturgis and I told him about what a great part of the world you find in the Black Hills of South Dakota. "I thought I was just going to pass through but I ended up staying three days and met some nice people who still send me messages on myspace."

"Hey I'm on myspace too. So what's your book about? Have any trouble getting rides."

"Not really. I have a hunch when I write about you and your buddy, it will be about the last ride I got."

He told me about his job driving around from town to town building and fixing cell towers. "Hey, this is the second crew of telecom nomads I met. The first was in Nevada. I had just spent a two days hunting with an Indian in Northern Nevada and a telecom crew passed me and the boss told the guy if he was bored he should pick me up. He dd and we had a great time. Just like you guys."

Though I had yet to meet his buddy Barry who was driving a few miles ahead of us.

"How you getting to Delaware from Hagerstown," he asked as we saw the sign saying it was just a few miles away.

"I don't know yet. Guess I'll check the map."

And soon Chad and Barry and I were in Hagerstown, checking their routes on their GPS. The shortest way was right through Baltimore, 60 miles away.

"Come on Barry, we're not doing anything else tonite. Might as well give Colin a ride to Baltimore."

Dang, that was great. Cause I was still in one of those places that went everywhere and nowhere at the same time.

Barry drove while Chad kept the heavy metal going in the front seat. These guys both close to 30 years old, loved that heavy metal.

"So what's different now about hitchhiking then when you were doing it back in the 70's," Barry asked.

"Bigger novelty now," I said. "I cannot remember the last time I saw a hitchhiker before this trip."

A few minutes later we were back to talking about heavy metal, and Baltimore, and where they were going to drop me off. The Baltimore Travel Center welcomed me.

Downtown Baltimore. Dark. Wet. Rainy. Maybe I could get the final ride of the trip without asking my brother to drive 50 miles to pick me up.The road was a few blocks away from this travel center. And the entrance ramp was narrow, and dangerous on about ten levels.

I was in the wrong part of town at the wrong time of night. So I did what I would have done 40 years ago: Called my big brother to rescue me. And he did.

POST SCRIPT

Finished the trip. Then -- while claiming to write this book -- took 6 months to live at my childhood friend Pat Ritchie's house in Hockessin, Delaware. Which is basically a beautiful house in the middle of the woods with a nice stream, a good dog, respectful kids, and a beautiful wife Derry who sure can cook.

I would gladly hitch around for a few more months for another six months of partying over there.

Made in the USA
Columbia, SC
10 September 2017